Living Parables

Living Parables

Today's Versions

Mark G. Boyer
and Corbin S. Cole

WIPF *&* STOCK · Eugene, Oregon

LIVING PARABLES
Today's Versions

Wipf & Stock
An Imprint of Wipf and Stock Publishers
199 W. 8th Ave., Suite 3
Eugene, OR 97401

www.wipfandstock.com

PAPERBACK ISBN: 978-1-7252-8580-4
HARDCOVER ISBN: 978-1-7252-8579-8
EBOOK ISBN: 978-1-7252-8581-1

11/09/20

Dedicated to
Shelbydog,
a living parable,
brindle-sparkling-in-the-sun red,
four-footed funny companion on the journey,
and a mystical burning bush in our midst—
an image of the Divine.

"Hear this, all you peoples;
give ear, all inhabitants of the world,
both low and high,
rich and poor together.
My mouth shall speak wisdom;
the meditation of my heart shall be understanding.
I will incline my ear to a proverb;
I will solve my riddle to the music of the harp."

—PS 49:1–4

"Give ear, O my people, to my teaching;
Incline your ears to the words of my mouth.
I will open my mouth in a parable;
I will utter dark sayings from of old,
things that we have heard and known,
that our ancestors have told us."

—PS 78:1–3

"From everyone to whom much has been given,
much will be required;
and from the one to whom much as been entrusted,
even more will be demanded."

—LUKE 12:48b

Contents

Abbreviations

BCE = Before the Common Era (same as BC = Before Christ)

CB (NT) = Christian Bible (New Testament)
    Heb = Letter to the Hebrews
    Luke = Luke's Gospel
    Mark = Mark's Gospel
    Matt = Matthew's Gospel

CE = Common Era (same as AD = *Anno Domini*, in the year of the Lord)

HB (OT) = Hebrew Bible (Old Testament)
    Judg = Judges
    Ps = Psalm
    2 Sam = Second Book of Samuel

OT (A) = Old Testament (Apocrypha)
    2 Esd = Second Book of Esdras

Introduction

LIVING PARABLES: TODAY'S VERSIONS is a book that presents parables in updated language and images. Biblical parables are culture
bound, that is, they are embedded in images that were well known
to a Jewish culture of the first century CE. Scott explains: "A sub-
stantial bar to making the parables applicable today is the great
distance between them and us. Jesus was a first-century, Jewish,
Galilean peasant, and his concerns, speech, and idioms belong to
that culture."[1] Griffin explains that "every single text in the Bible
was composed in a cultural milieu very different and far removed
from ours today."[2] The ancient images found in parables carried
meaning that is lost on modern audiences. A simple example will
suffice. In the Jewish world of the first century, leaven or yeast was
considered to be corrupt because people did not understand how
bacteria worked. That is why on the most important day of the
year—Passover—bread had to be unleavened, uncorrupted. Today,
no one thinks of yeast or leaven in that way. We know that if we
want bread dough to rise, we need to put yeast in it. Therefore,
what image might Jesus use today that carries some of the same
cultural connotations that yeast or leaven carried in his world?
Might he speak about Ebola virus, COVID-19 (coronavirus), or

1. Scott, "Living," 15.
2. Griffin, "Reading the Bible," 7.

radioactivity? Those images carry the same negativity that yeast or leaven bore in his world but is unavailable to ours. This book contains parables found in the Christian Bible (New Testament)—and a few located in the Hebrew Bible (Old Testament)—in a form that Jesus might tell today. We are able to do this because "the parables do invoke universal themes."[3]

The Greek word *parable*—meaning to throw together, to put beside, to compare—is the translation of the Hebrew word *masal*—meaning a wise saying, a maxim, or a taunt song. Biblical scholars cannot agree on how many parables there are because some do not consider some of Jesus' stories as parables. A search of the *New Revised Standard Version* of the Bible used in this work, presents over seventy matches for the word *parable*. In this book we do not make distinctions between parables (fictive stories) employing similes (using the words *like* or *as*), and metaphors (a comparison of one thing to another) because that is not our objective. After careful study of what the parable meant to the original audience, we rewrite it with the intent of capturing it in language for today's reader or listener. Jesus spoke parables in Aramaic; gospel writers recorded parables in Greek; and you are reading them in English. As anyone who speaks another language knows, it is near impossible to capture the meaning of words in one language by translating them into another. Something cultural is lost, and something else cultural is gained. For example, the Greek word *zume* used to be translated into English as *leaven* or *sour dough*. Since many people today do not know what leaven or sour dough is, the translated word becomes *yeast*. Leaven, sour dough, and yeast each capture some of the meaning of *zume*, and each lose some of the meaning of *zume*. Furthermore, each word is bound to a specific culture or subculture in the English-speaking world. Even some English-speakers may not know what yeast is! Using an image borrowed from Rohr, we can say that our bandwidth of parabolic access to the Bible has been severely narrowed.[4]

---

3. Scott, "Living," 15.
4. Rohr, "Many Ways."

Attempting to define the word *parable* is as varied as those proposing definitions. A parable can be a succinct, didactic story that illustrates a lesson to be learned. It can be a short fictitious story that illustrates a moral attitude or a religious principle. Sometimes, a parable is a short allegorical story designed to illustrate or teach some truth. Those definitions can easily be found almost anywhere. O'Loughlin writes, "A parable . . . is a glimpse into a mythic world where we can see what cannot be seen and experience what is beyond experience."[5] Galston writes about "understanding parables as a paradoxical glimpse at what could have been but wasn't and might yet be but isn't."[6] Galston states that a parable calls us both "from another world and to another world, one that can be and maybe even should be." He adds, "The parables give glimpses of this alternative. . . ."[7] They continually ask people to face the now and to re-imagine a future.

Hall, quoting C. H. Dodd, presents the simplest definition of the meaning of the word *parable*. "The parable is a metaphor or simile drawn from nature or common life, arresting the hearer by its vividness or strangeness, and leaving the mind in sufficient doubt about its precise application to tease it into active thought."[8] As noted above, *parable* means to throw together, to put beside, and to compare. Thus, Hall states that "parables take two discreet and not entirely comparable objects drawn from nature or common life and put them into relationship with each other. The metaphorical nature of parables gives them the ability to surprise and shock."[9] Such is the example of the kingdom of heaven being like yeast that a woman took and mixed in with three measures of four until all of it was leavened (Matt 13:33; Luke 13:21). Because we do not understand the culture out of which this parable emerged, we end up taming it. The kingdom of heaven is like corruption or decay that a woman—not a man!—hides in three—the biblical number referencing

5. O'Loughlin, *Eating Together*, 109.
6. Galston, "Dispatches," 29.
7. Galston, "Dispatches," 29.
8. Hall, "Jesus: God's Story," 12.
9. Hall, "Jesus: God's Story," 12.

God—measures (a bushel basket) of flour until the whole batch is contaminated! Once we know that yeast was understood to be a corruptive agent, and it is placed in relationship to God's reign, we cannot help but grasp the parable in a new way. Reading the one-verse text "inevitably seems to elicit strong reactions: confusion or distrust, recognition or embrace," states Windley-Daust.[10]

Griffin offers us an in-depth explanation of metaphor and how it works in parables:

> [A] metaphor is one thing used in a phrase or sentence as an imaginative reference for another thing. It is a figurative reference that communicates a similarity-in-difference between them. . . . It is possible for anything to be used as a metaphor. All that is required is an imagination that can capture the meaning of an experience or other aspect of something that is readily familiar to both speaker and listener. The meaning is perceived when heard with an equally imaginative ear. The parables of Jesus are a prime example of metaphorical references. The meaning is disclosed in the paradoxical juxtaposition of references.[11]

Windley-Daust argues that the purpose of the juxtaposition of references in parables is to engage the hearer. "It does not leave most people disengaged," she writes.

> The reactions lead to questions—allowing God to work through your thought process—but beyond it as well. In our culture, parabolic language is a way of turning our received understandings of relationships on their head. Parables have a way of turning our expectations inside, outside, upside down, and you land in a place that is familiar but new, a humble spot of in-breaking revelation.[12]

In order for parables to challenge expectations, they must be understood in their time, place, culture—milieu. That is what we attempt to do in this book. We do not present the results of exegesis as biblical scholars do. We take the results and apply them to the

---

10. Windley-Daust, "A Literature of Encounter?" 10.
11. Griffin, "Reading the Bible," 6.
12. Windley-Daust, "A Literature of Encounter?" 10–11.

culture in which we live. We search for well-known images that challenge our expectations in order to undo the taming that the parables have undergone. Instead of presenting yeast, we present radioactivity, virus, radon gas, etc.

Griffin states that parables "were undoubtedly designed to be mythic or imaginative, maybe even fanciful, in order to communicate with the readers and invite them to identify with the story as if they were participants."[13] This can only occur if the hearers of the parables experience their expectations being turned upside down. When this happens, spiritual transformation occurs in the hearer. That is why the gospel narrators state that Jesus did not speak except in parables (Mark 4:34; Matt 13:34). Of course, the narrators contradict themselves by writing about other things Jesus said and did, making the gospels parables! Nevertheless, Jesus' parables are some of the ways he taught about spirituality, whose goal is transformation. This can be gleaned easily by noticing his emphasis on growth and development in his parables. Rayas refers to this as "crossing borders." He explains, ". . . [I]n crossing borders we lose something and gain something; we give up something to get something."[14]

When unlike images are thrown together, put beside each other, or compared, the hearer is made aware of—transformed by—the presence of God. Many of Jesus' parables begin by declaring that the kingdom of God, the kingdom of heaven, the reign of God, or the empire of God is like something that shakes the hearer's usual way of thinking. Nowhere does Jesus explain what the kingdom, reign, or empire of God is. According to Luke's Gospel, he merely states, ". . . [T]he kingdom of God is among you"[15] (Luke 17:21); or ". . . [T]he Kingdom of God is in your midst";[16] or "God's kingdom is here with you."[17] Saying the kingdom of God is like yeast doesn't transform the hearers of our culture. Saying the

13. Griffin, "Reading the Bible," 7.

14. Rayas, "Discipleship," 37

15. *Access Bible*, NT, 114.

16. NT: *St. Paul Edition*, 206.

17. *Contemporary English Version*, 1252.

reign of God is like rat poison might! Saying the empire of God is like antifreeze might! Thinking differently about God means one is being transformed. A person is in the presence of God, and all he or she can do is pray. Rohr makes clear that "prayer is not saying words or thinking thoughts" although such may occur after really hearing a parable. "It is, rather, a stance. It's a way of living in the Presence, living in awareness of the Presence, and even joining the Presence."[18] Parables, if they work, are the matches that start the fire. "What is happening is God living in us, with us, and through us as our unique manifestation of love. And each one of us is a bit different because the forms of love are infinite."[19] One hurdle over which Jesus seemed to have jumped was the division between the sacred and the secular. His parables take secular images and compare them to his sacred God. "Sacred and secular are not opposites," states Griffin. "They are complementary."[20] Reading and hearing modern parables can unleash our imaginations "to behold horizons of meaning heretofore not recognized but waiting to come to light."[21]

Ben-Shahar refers to "horizons of meaning" as spiritual well-being. He states, ". . . [S]piritual well-being refers to the importance of finding a sense of purpose and meaning in life, as well as to elevating ordinary experiences into extraordinary ones through mindful presence."[22] That is exactly what parables are designed to do. They take something ordinary and compare it to something extraordinary or vice-versa in order to spur the hearer deeper into transformation. Jesus spent a lot of his ministry telling parables about the kingdom, the reign, and the empire of God. Jesus is not the topic of parables, and parables do not imagine a perfect world. Nevertheless, Jesus presents a different view of the God hidden in his parables. According to gospel writers, often he ended them by stating, "Let anyone with ears to hear listen!" (Mark 4:9, 23; 7:15;

18. Rohr, "Loving."
19. Rohr, "Loving."
20. Griffin, "Reading the Bible," 20.
21. Griffin, "Reading the Bible," 20.
22. Ben-Shahar, "Five Questions," 104.

Matt 11:15, 13:9, 43; Luke 8:8; 14:35) In other words, he invited listeners to think over the parables and draw their own conclusions that let the parables explode, that let them undermine their everyday assumptions, while knowing that there is always the risk that the parables might be misunderstood or rejected. If the parables work, God is disclosed by Jesus. If our rewritten versions of Jesus' parables work, the hidden God may be disclosed to you.

There are two kinds of parables. The first is known as an aphorism, "which can be defined as a short saying with two characteristics: first, its meaning is unclear on its surface, and second, it challenges the accepted view of things."[23] An aphorism "invites us to follow our hunches that things are not always as they seem to be and the sometimes there is a richer and more humane—if more difficult—truth that is incompatible with what convention, convenience, and conformity present as common sense."[24] In the CB (NT), the yeast parable and the mustard seed parable are examples of aphorisms. The second type of parable is narrative; it is "a story or an account of a sequence of events in the order in which they happened."[25] Narrative parables leave the hearer wondering what action he or she should take. In the CB (NT), the good Samaritan and the lost (prodigal) son are examples of narrative parables.

No matter whether they be aphorisms or narrative, parables are supposed "to open a window in the wall of our imagination, a window through which we might get a glimpse of what the world could be like if God was running it, that frightening yet fascinating possibility Jesus called the empire of God."[26] Scott aptly summarizes what we present in this book:

> The parable is always a counterweight to the default world, and as such it imagines a counterweighted God. The God Jesus hides in the parables identifies with a polluted world, not the world of the temple; Adonai's presence is discovered in absence, not apocalyptic revenge;

23. Miller, "Inside(r)s and Outside(r)s," 10.
24. Miller, "Inside(r)s and Outside(r)s," 10.
25. *Encarta*, 1203.
26. Miller, "Inside(r)s and Outside(r)s," 11.

and G-d's empire is based not on shame and honor, not patron and client, not contest—but on cooperation. The risk in such a counterweighted world is that the power of other empires is mighty indeed. Since the counter-world of the parable is always an imagined world, the real world is always there, always threatening to destroy the world of imagination.[27]

We hope that you will find a counterweighted God in our imagined parables and get a glimpse of God's kingdom, reign, or empire that moves you to ever further transformation.

This Book

Living Parables: Today's Versions contains five chapters. The first three are organized according to the gospels in the CB (NT): Matthew, Mark, and Luke. The last two contain other biblical parables from the HB (OT) and the OT (A) and modern parables that are not like those found in biblical literature. Within each of the first three chapters are the parables found in the order in which they appear in the specific gospel. The traditional name for the parable—such as the lost sheep—has been retained, and the notation of where the parable can be found in the specific gospel—such as Luke 15:3–7—is given. We recommend that you read the original parable along with any notes your Bible provides before reading the modern versions we present. Depending on the specific parable, there may be other versions of it in other gospels—such as the mustard seed (Mark 4:30–32; Matt 13:31–32; Luke 13:18–19)—and we usually present several modern versions of it for your consideration. If you understand the modern parable, spend time with it, reflecting on its meaning and appropriating it for your spiritual growth. If you do not understand the modern parable, move on to the next one.

The fourth chapter presents parables not found in the gospels. As for the gospel parables, we present these in the order in which they appear in biblical books. Likewise, the traditional name for

27. Scott, "Living," 19.

the parable has been retained, and the notation of where the parable can be found in the Bible is given. The fifth chapter presents two types—aphorisms and narrative parables—that we have found in various sources. Some of these come from written texts, but the majority were spoken by friends or by one of us. The reader will notice that throughout the chapters of this book infrequently there is a footnote attached to a rewritten parable indicating the person who wrote it. The name indicates a former student of Mark Boyer, who in the fall semester of 1991 in his Literature and World of the New Testament class gave extra credit to students who rewrote parables with the promise that good ones might be included in a book some day.

Biblical Notes

The Bible is divided into two parts: The Hebrew Bible (Old Testament) and the Christian Bible (New Testament). The Hebrew Bible consists of thirty-nine named books, written roughly between 1200 and 164 BCE, accepted by Jews and Protestants as Holy Scripture. The Old Testament also contains those thirty-nine books plus seven to fifteen more named books or parts of books called the Apocrypha or the Deuterocanonical Books; the Old Testament is accepted by Catholics and several other Christian denominations as Holy Scripture. The Christian Bible, consisting of twenty-seven named books, written between 50 and 115 CE, is also called the New Testament; it is accepted by Christians as Holy Scripture. Thus, in this work:

- Hebrew Bible (Old Testament), abbreviated HB (OT), indicates that a book is found both in the Hebrew Bible and the Old Testament;

- Old Testament (Apocrypha), abbreviated OT (A), indicates that a book is found only in the Old Testament Apocrypha and not in the Hebrew Bible;

- and Christian Bible (New Testament), abbreviated CB (NT),
  indicates that a book is found only in the Christian Bible or
  New Testament.

In notating biblical texts, the first number refers to the chapter in the book, and the second number refers to the verse within the chapter. Thus, HB (OT) Isa 7:11 means that the quotation comes from Isaiah, chapter 7, verse 11. OT (A) Sirach 39:30 means that the quotation comes from Sirach, chapter 39, verse 30. CB (NT) Mark 6:2 means that the quotation comes from Mark's Gospel, chapter 6, verse 2. When more than one sentence appears in a verse, the letters a, b, c, etc. indicate the sentence being referenced in the verse. Thus, HB (OT) 2 Kgs 1:6a means that the quotation comes from the Second Book of Kings, chapter 1, verse 6, sentence 1. Also, poetry, such as the Psalms, may be noted using the letters a, b, c, etc. to indicate the lines being used. Thus, Psalm 16:4a refers to the first line of verse 4 of Psalm 16; there are two more lines of verse 4: b and c.

Biblical Presuppositions

The HB (OT) begins as stories passed on by word of mouth from one person to another. Sometime during the oral transmission stage, authors decide to collect the oral stories and write them. A change occurs immediately when oral stories are written. One does not tell a story the same way one writes a story. Repetition and correction occur in oral story-telling. Except for future emendations by copyists, single statements by characters and plot structure guides dominate written stories.

In the CB (NT) the oldest gospel is Mark's account of Jesus' victory. The author of Matthew's Gospel copied and shortened about eighty percent of Mark's material into his book and then added other stories to make the work longer. The author of Luke's Gospel copied and shortened about fifty percent of Mark's material into his orderly account and then added other stories to make the work much longer. Mark's Gospel begins as oral story-telling, lasting for about forty years in that form. An unidentified author, called Mark for the sake of convenience, collects the oral stories, sets a plot, and writes the first gospel around 70 CE. Because Jesus was expected to return soon, no one had thought about recording what he had said and done until Mark came along and realized that he was not returning as quickly as had been thought. About ten years after Mark finished his gospel, Matthew needed to adopt Mark's narrative—originally intended for a peasant Gentile readership—to a Jewish audience. And about twenty years after Mark finished his gospel, Luke needed to adapt Mark's poor Gentile-intended work for a rich, upper class, urban, Gentile readership.

In addition to the material the authors of Matthew's Gospel and Luke's Gospel copied from Mark's Gospel, both the author of Matthew's Gospel and the author of Luke's Gospel had another common source; this source is named Q by biblical scholars. Q is the abbreviation for *Quelle*, a German word meaning *source*. In general, the source seems to be sayings of Jesus which each author placed into narratives he deemed appropriate. Thus, when a saying like Matthew 5:3 and Luke 6:20 are almost identical in wording, biblical scholars consider the source of the saying to be Q. Or, for example, the short parable known as the leaven, found in Matthew 13:33 and Luke 13:20–21, is Q material.

Furthermore, gospels were not first intended to be read privately as is done today. They were meant to be heard in a group. The very low rate of literacy in the first century would have never dictated many copies of texts since most people could not read, and their standard practice was to listen to another tell or read the stories to them. Thus, what began as oral story-telling passed on by word of mouth became written story-telling preserved in gospels. A careful reading of Mark's Gospel will reveal the orality still embedded in the text, especially evident in the repetition of words and the organization of stories in three parts. In rewriting Mark, Matthew and Luke remove the last traces of oral story-telling.

Specifically concerning parables, we can say that Jesus told parables. Parables were born in orality. What Jesus said may or may not be what the gospel writers recorded, because we do not hear what a person says; we hear what we think a person says. This is true for one-sentence aphorisms and even truer for long narrative parables. Each gospel author placed parables in his narrative where he determined they fit best. Matthew and Luke often provide a setting different from the setting for parables they found in Mark's Gospel. They often group parables together because they think they convey the same or similar theme. Furthermore, gospel writers often provide some interpretation of the parable; this is especially true of Luke, who often writes an introduction for a parable, a conclusion, or both. We do not include such interpretations in our rewritten parables unless it is absolutely necessary for context. In other words, we attempt to let the parable stand alone and challenge the reader to interpret it. Because there was no one following Jesus with a cell phone to record his words, we have only the second-hand witness of written texts embedded in the synoptic gospels (Mark, Matthew, and Luke). There are other sources for parables, such as the Gospel of Thomas, but we do not rewrite any of the parables found in it. This books focuses on the parables found in the synoptic gospels (there are no parables in John's Gospel) and a very few that are found in the HB (OT) and OT (A).

Parables Cross Referenced

For your convenience, we provide the following list of cross-referenced parables from the synoptic gospels. When a parable occurs in all three gospels, the list follows the order of Mark, Matthew, and then Luke. When it is a Q parable, found in both Matthew and Luke but not in Mark, it follows the order of Matthew and then Luke.

> Patches and Wineskins: Mark 2:21–22, Matt 9:16–17, Luke 5:36–39
>
> House Building: Matt 7:24–27, Luke 6:47–49
>
> Blind Leading the Blind: Matt 15:10–20, Luke 6:39–42
>
> Sower and Seed: Mark 4:3–9, Matt 13:3–9, Luke 8:4–8

Lamp: Mark 4:21–23, Luke 8:16

Mustard Seed: Mark 4:30–32, Matt 13:31–32, Luke 13:18–19

Leaven (Yeast): Matt 13:33, Luke 13:20–21

Lost Sheep: Matt 18:12–13, Luke 15:3–7

Vineyard: Mark 12:1–9, Matt 21:33–41, Luke 20:9–16

Talents/Pounds: Matt 25:14–30, Luke 19:11–27

Our goal is to rewrite the parables using modern images for a contemporary culture that capture the impact of some of the original images for an ancient Jewish culture. We also provide some parables whose origin is our culture; our hope is that they will prompt the reader to stop and reflect. You, the reader, will be the judge of how well we have achieved our goal.

Mark G. Boyer
Corbin S. Cole

Parables in Matthew's Gospel

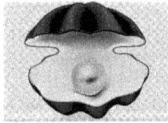

House Building

(Matt 7:24–27)

JESUS SAID: "EVERYONE WHO hears these words of mine and acts on them will be like a wise contractor who built his house on a concrete foundation. The rain fell, the floods came, and the winds blew and beat on that house, but it did not fall, because it had been founded on concrete. And everyone who hears these words of mine and does not act on them will be like a foolish contractor who built his house on soil. The rain fell, and the floods came, and the winds blew and beat against that house, and it fell—and great was its fall."

Jesus said: "Everyone who hears these words of mine and acts on them will be like a wise contractor who, living in a tornado zone, built a shelter out of thick concrete. The rain fell, the floods came, and the winds blew, and a tornado dipped down out of the clouds and hit that shelter, but it did not fall, because it had been founded on thick concrete. And everyone who hears these words of mine and does not act on them will be like a foolish contractor who, living in a tornado zone, built a shelter out of wood. The rain fell, and the floods came, and the winds blew, and a tornado dipped down out of the clouds and hit that shelter, and it was shredded into many tiny pieces and blown away."

Jesus said: "Everyone who hears these words of mine and acts on them will be like a wise contractor who, living in a hurricane zone, built a shelter out of thick concrete. The rain fell, the floods came, and the winds blew, and a hurricane hit that shelter, but it did not fall, because it had been founded on thick concrete. And everyone who hears these words of mine and does not act on them will be like a foolish contractor who, living in a hurricane zone, built a shelter out of wood. The rain fell, and the floods came, and the winds blew, and a hurricane hit that shelter, and it was shredded into many tiny pieces and blown away."

Jesus said: "Everyone who hears these words of mine and acts on them will be like a wise couple from Missouri who chose to build their house on a concrete foundation. The rain fell, flash floods came, and Midwest tornadoes blew and beat on the house, but it did not fall because it was built on concrete. And everyone who hears these words of mine and does not act on them will be like a foolish couple from Missouri who built their house on soil. The rain fell, flash floods came, and tornadoes blew and beat against that house, and it fell—and it was a great fall!"

Jesus said: "Everyone who hears these words of mine and acts on them will be like a wise contractor in Australia who built homes out of steel and concrete. The land dried up, the summer came, and a massive wildfire broke out, but the house did not fall, for it was built to withstand the flames. And everyone who hears these words of mine and does not act on them will be like a foolish contractor in Australia who built his homes completely out of wood. The land dried up, the summer came, and a massive wildfire broke out and consumed the house and it burned to the ground—and it was a great disaster!"

Patches and Wineskins

(Matt 9:16–17)

Jesus told the disciples of the Dalai Lama, who had asked him about the lack of fasting of his disciples: "No teacher takes a sticker off a student's old homework assignment and puts it on a new one, for the sticker won't stay attached and pulls away from the later assignment, and is lost among the papers on the teacher's desk. Neither is an iron-on patch put on old jeans; otherwise, the patch comes off in the wash, and the jeans are torn more, and the patch is destroyed; but a new iron-on patch is put on a new pair of jeans, and so both are preserved.

Jesus told the disciples of the Dalai Lama, who had asked him about the lack of fasting of his disciples: "No one puts a pair of rusty strings on a brand-new guitar, for the strings will sound bad, break, and may damage the guitar. Neither is a new guitar put into an old non-protective case for travel; otherwise the case will be opened after a day of airline travel and the new guitar will be destroyed; but a new guitar is put into a new protective case, and so both are preserved.

Jesus told the disciples of the Dalai Lama, who had asked him about the lack of fasting of his disciples: "No one puts a piece of moldy fruit in a bowl of fresh fruit, for the mold will spread and the entire bowl of fruit will be tainted. Neither is fresh fruit put into an old unwashed storage bin; otherwise, the crop will be infected with mold and bugs, and the entire bin of fruit will be lost; but fresh fruit is put into a clean bowl with other fresh fruit or stored in a clean bin, and all fruit is preserved.

Sower and Seed

(Matt 13:3–9)

Jesus told the crowd on the beach many things in parables, saying: "Listen! A Kansas farmer drove his tractor into a freshly plowed field in the autumn to plant winter wheat. And as he drove the tractor and planter up one row and down the other, some winter wheat seeds fell on the road, and the crows came and ate them. Other seeds fell on the gravely ground, where they did not have much soil, and they sprang up quickly in the spring when the snow melted, since they had no depth of soil. But when the warm spring sun rose, they were scorched; and since they had no root, they withered away. Other winter wheat seeds fell among the wild blackberry canes growing near the edge of the field, and the wild blackberry canes blossomed and leafed and choked them. Other winter wheat seeds fell on good soil and brought forth grain, some a hundred bushels per acre, some sixty, some thirty. Let anyone with ears listen!"

Jesus told the crowd on the beach many things in parables, saying: "Listen! A Nebraska farmer went out to sow corn seed in his newly-plowed field. And as he drove his tractor with the planter be-hind, some corn seeds fell on the asphalt road, and the robins came and ate them. Other corn seeds fell on gravely ground, where they did not have much soil, and they sprang up quickly after the first spring rain, since they had no depth of soil. But when the clouds cleared and the hot sun shown, they were scorched, and since they had no root, they withered away. Other corn seeds fell among brush growing along the fence enclosing the field, and the brush grew up and choked them. Other corn seeds fell on good soil and brought forth large ears of corn, some a thousand bushels per acre, some six hundred, some three hundred. Let anyone with ears listen!"

Jesus told the crowd on the beach many things in parables, saying: "Listen! A gardener went out to plant lotus seeds in her water garden. As she worked, some seeds fell on the bank of the pond, and the birds ate them for an easy meal. Other seeds fell in the rocky shallows of the pond and sprang up quickly because they were immersed in water; yet when the sun came up the next day, they were burned up, and because they had no roots, they withered away. Other seeds fell in deep water, and were drowned. Other seeds fell over mud in adequate water and blossomed into beautiful lotus flowers. Let anyone with ears to hear listen!"

Jesus told the crowd on the beach many things in parables, saying: "Listen! An orphanage was placing children with families.

As the adoption process played out, some children were placed with abusive families, never getting a chance to succeed in life. Other children were placed with loving families and flourished, only to be moved a few months later and have their hopes wither away. Some children were placed in extremely strict homes, where their spirits were suffocated and they weren't equipped for their adult lives. Other children were placed in loving, caring homes, which enabled them to flourish throughout their lives. Let anyone with ears able to hear listen!"

Once upon a time there were three Bible students who were given a CD by their teacher. The CD featured a televangelist broadcast; the students were told to take the CD home, watch it, and learn biblical lessons from it. Each took home a copy of the CD and proceeded to begin to watch it. The first was disturbed and distracted by noises outside. Therefore, he never understood the meaning of the CD because he did not pay close attention to it. The second began watching the CD and learning from it, but her cell phone rang. Instead of quickly ending the call and finishing the CD, she forgot all about it and became engrossed in the conversation with her friend. But the third student turned off his cell phone and concentrated on the CD and understood what the televangelist was communication. He then became so happy and excited about what he learned that he made copies of the CD for his friends and encouraged them to watch it and to learn from it.[1]

A teacher was preparing students for a test with a lecture. As the teacher taught, some of the students did not comprehend the meaning of the lecture; so they lost interest quickly. Others understood at once, but became bored with the lecture and eventually lost interest also. Some of the students listened to the lecture, but they became distracted easily and didn't hear all that they needed to understand clearly. The last group of students understood the lecture, passed the test, and got an A for the course. The students who really want to learn will learn![2]

---

1. McGinnis, "Literature."
2. Ridenhour, "Literature."

Wheat and Weeds

(Matt 13:24–30)

Jesus told another parable: "The kingdom of heaven may be compared to a composer who completed a symphony; but before publication an enemy composer changed the notes in one of the symphony's movements. So when the conductor practiced the symphony with his orchestra, the unknown notes appeared. And the conductor came to the composer and said to him, 'Did you not place better notes in your symphony? Where then did these strange notes come from?' He answered, 'An enemy composer has done this.' The conductor said to him, 'Then, do you want me to remove those notes from the symphony?' But the composer replied, 'No; for in removing the unknown notes you would remove some of the original notes with them. Let both of them be played together until the symphony is finished; after the listeners' applause I will tell the first violinist, Collect all the orchestra's booklets, remove the movement that has been altered, and bind the sheets of music in bundles to be burned, but gather the rest of booklets for storage in the music archives.'"

Jesus told another parable: "The kingdom of heaven may be compared to the National Football League draft, when teams choose rookies for their season; but before new players played, they were tested by the team coaches. So, when the assistant coach noted that a rookie was not a good player, he went to the head coach and said to him, 'Sir, did you not draft good players? Where then did this uncoordinated rookie come from?' He answered, 'An enemy coach has done this.' The assistant coach said to him, 'Then, do you want me to fire the rookie?' But the head coach replied, 'No; for in firing the rookie you would remove some of our potential plays. Let all the rookies play together until the game is finished; after the final score, I will tell the general manager, Collect all the players' statistics and fire the players who did not meet our expectations; but gather together the rest of the rookies to sign contracts for the next five years.'"

Jesus told another parable: "The kingdom of heaven may be compared to a lake with native mussels; but someone launched a boat infected with zebra mussels into the lake. So when the conservation agent came to inspect the lake, the zebra mussels appeared. And the agent came to the conservation director and said to him, 'Boss, did you not see native mussels in the lake? Where then did these zebra mussels come from?' He answered, 'An enemy boater has done this.' The agent said to him, 'Then, do you want me to remove those zebra mussels from the lake?' But the director replied, 'No; for in removing the zebra mussels you would remove some of the native mussels with them. Let both of them grow together until the end of the boating season; I will tell all the agents, Collect all the mussels from the lake and first put the zebra mussels into containers to be burned, but return the native mussels to the lake to flourish.'"

Jesus told another parable: "The kingdom of heaven may be compared to a highway road crew that planted clover along the sides of the road to stop erosion; but residents living in that area planted kudzu. So when the director of state highways visited the site, he noticed the kudzu growing over the clover. And the director went to the road crew manager and said to him, 'Sir, did you not plant clover to control erosion along that highway? Where then did the kudzu come from?' He answered, 'The enemy residents living in the area did this.' The manager said to him, 'Then, do you want me to remove the kudzu?' But the director replied, 'No; for in removing the kudzu you would remove the clover too. Let both of them grow together until the fall; then, I will tell the road crew, "Collect all the invasive, climbing, coiling, and trailing kudzu first and pile the vines to be burned, but gather the clover, divide the clumps, and replant it all along the highway."'"

Jesus told another parable: "The kingdom of heaven may be compared to a nursery arborist who planted pine, dogwood, maple, redbud, oak, and hickory trees on his forty acres of property in the autumn; but while he was away, an enemy came and plated Bradford pear trees among the other trees, and then went away. So when spring came and the trees began to produce leaves, the white pear blossoms appeared as well. And the arborist's employees came and said to him, 'Boss, did you not plant only native trees on your nursery property? Where then did these Bradford pear trees come from?' He answered, 'An enemy has done this.' The employees said to him, 'Then, do you want us to go and gather them?' But the arborist replied, 'No; for in gathering the Bradford pears you would uproot the pine, dogwood, maple, redbud, oak, and hickory trees along with them. Let all the trees grow together in the nursery until the autumn; and at autumn I will tell the woodsmen, 'Cut the Bradford pears first and stack them on a pile to be burned, but spread manure and fertilizer on all the rest.''

Jesus told another parable: "The kingdom of heaven is like this: An agri-technician—we used to call him a farmer—went out to his field one day and sowed terrific wheat seeds. These seeds were the really good stuff. They were used for making bread at upscale gourmet Jerusalem restaurants. Well, this agri-technician, in spite of being a really terrific guy—somewhat like yours truly—had an enemy! Now this enemy dude sneaked into the field at night when everybody was watching late night TV and sowed weed seeds! As my uncle from Brooklyn used to declare, 'The nerve of that guy!' Well, both kinds of seeds came up side by side—wheat and weeds. They didn't get along very well, of course, and it would have gotten ugly if they had been able to swing their leaves at each other. Fortunately, plants cannot do that! One day the agri-technician's foreman came to him and said, 'Yo, boss! Didn't you sow the good stuff out there in yonder wheat field?' And the boss replied, 'Of course. I care enough to seed the very best.' So, the foreman said, 'Well, I'll be doggoned if I can figure out from where all the weeds are coming.' The agri-technician thought a moment and said, 'An enemy has done this!' To which the foreman replied, 'No duh, Sherlock!' A couple of seconds later the foreman had an idea: 'Tell you what, boss man. How about I mosey out there to those weeds and terminate them with Roundup?' The wheat plants thought that was a spiffy idea, while the weeds were extremely negative about it. But the boss said, 'No! If you spray the weeds, you might also spray the wheat with them. Let them grow together until harvest. Then I'll tell the harvesters to gather the weeds and make the biggest, baddest, hottest bonfire this country's every seen. After that, we'll bring the wheat into the silo and make French bread and funnel cakes!'"[3]

In a small suburb outside of Los Angeles there was a little town with one public school. This being such a small town with little excitement, things usually ran pretty smoothly. However, Carlos, a big drug lord in LA, saw much potential by moving some of his business into the little town. So he sent some of his gang members to establish residency and enroll in school so he could sell drugs to the students. Slowly, but surely, a few of the students got involved with Carlos's gang and began using drugs. When the sheriff heard about this, he was angry, but he did not arrest any of the gang members. Instead, he notified the Los Angeles Police Department Drug Enforcement Office, which conducted an investigation in the school in order to gather evidence against the gang. During the investigation, the sheriff waited patiently, knowing that Carlos would pay for what he had done. Sure enough, when the investigation was complete, Carlos and his gang members were arrested and given prison sentences by a judge.[4]

Mustard Seed

(Matt 13:31–32)

Jesus put before his disciples another parable: "The kingdom of heaven is like a chive seed that someone took and sowed in his field; it is one of the smallest of all the seeds, but when it has grown it is the greatest of shrubs and becomes a tree, so that the birds of the air come and make nests in its branches."

Jesus put before his disciples another parable: "The kingdom of heaven is like an acorn that someone took and planted in his field; it is one of the smallest of all the seeds, but when it has grown it is the greatest of brush and becomes a tree, so that the birds of the air come and make nests in its branches."

3. Adapted from Auer, "Darnel and Tares," 38–39.
4. McGinnis, "Literature."

Jesus put before his disciples another parable: "The kingdom of heaven is like a fertilized egg within a mother's womb; it is a tiny egg, but when it has grown, it becomes a human being with the ability to nurture others, just as it was once nurtured."

Jesus put before his disciples another parable: "The kingdom of heaven is like a microscopic singularity that is continually expanding. It is the smallest of substances, but when it has grown, it is a great substance; it is the universe as we know it. And it houses all the stars, planets, and life within its reach."

Leaven (Yeast)

(Matt 13:33)

Jesus told another parable: "The kingdom of heaven is like the atomic bomb that Lady Liberty secretly dropped on Hiroshima and Nagasaki with the force of three megatons of trinitrotoluene (TNT) until the cities were totally radiated."

Jesus told another parable: "The kingdom of heaven is like an atom that a female physicist took and crushed in the Large Hadron Collider for three seconds until a large explosion occurred."

Jesus told another parable: "The kingdom of heaven is like the single bullet that a woman fired from her rifle that sparked three thousand other soldiers to fire until all the enemy were dead."

Jesus told another parable: "The kingdom of heaven is like yeast added by a female vintner to a vat of grape juice until all the sugars were turned into alcohol."

Jesus told another parable: "The kingdom of heaven is like the shot heard around the world that killed Archduke Ferdinand of Austria until World War I began."

Jesus told another parable: "The kingdom of heaven is like a female factory president who releases polluted water into the river until all the fish are dead."

Jesus told another parable: "The kingdom of heaven is like a manufacturer who releases polluted air into the city three times a day until the residents of the whole city have asthma."

Jesus told another parable: "The kingdom of heaven is like three tons of plastic dumped into the ocean until the whole sea is polluted."

Jesus told another parable: "The kingdom of heaven is like drugs which a female pusher gave to three million children until they were all hooked."

Jesus told another parable: "The kingdom of heaven is like knowledge which a female teacher imparted to three students until all three were infected with truth."

Jesus told another parable: "The kingdom of heaven is like a virus which, when released from a woman's sneeze, spreads to three hundred people until all are ill."

Jesus told another parable: "The kingdom of heaven is like a vial of very contagious germ-warfare bacteria which, when accidentally placed in the garbage bin by a female scientist, infected three hundred people who came into contact with it."

Jesus told another parable: "The kingdom of heaven is like an architect's thought used to create blue prints, which guide the construction of a skyscraper in which three thousand people dwell."

Jesus told another parable: "The kingdom of heaven is like a rancid bag of garbage which a woman threw into the trash bin until all three other bags in the bin were stinking."

Jesus told another parable: "The kingdom of heaven is like a floor in a dance hall which gives way to three hundred female dancers until all fall through to the basement."

Treasure Hidden in a Field

(Matt 13:44)

The kingdom of heaven is like a rare coin hidden in a friend's back yard, which someone found with his metal detector and hid; then in his joy he goes and sells his house and lot and buys the house and lot of his friend.

The kingdom of heaven is like money hidden in a wall which a contractor, who was renovating an old house, found and hid;

then in his joy he goes and sells his own house and bought the house he was renovating.

The kingdom of heaven is like a diamond hidden in property bordering Crater of Diamonds State Park in Arkansas which someone found and hid; then in his joy he goes and sells all that he has and buys that property.

The kingdom of heaven is like Civil War items—rifle, chest of coins, and skeleton—hidden in a cave, which someone found and told no one about; then in his joy he goes and sells all that he has and buys the land upon which the cave is located.

The kingdom of heaven is like a gold nugget hidden in a stream which someone found and hid; then in his joy he goes and sells all that he has and buys that claim and those on either side of it.

Pearl of Great Price

(Matt 13:45–46)

Again, the kingdom of heaven is like a merchant in search of fine diamonds; on finding one large stone of great value, he went and sold all that he had and bought it.

Again, the kingdom of heaven is a like a merchant in search of very rare Lladro porcelain; on finding one statue of great value, he went and sold all that he had and bought it.

Again, the kingdom of heaven is a like a merchant in search of rare books; on finding one with $1200 hidden in its pages, he bought it for one dollar.

Again, the kingdom of heaven is like a musician in search of well-crafted instruments; on finding a hand-made Gibson guitar of great value, he went and sold all his other instruments and bought it.

Dragnet

(Matt 13:47–50)

Again, the kingdom of heaven is like a community garage sale whose members displayed many different items on multiple tables; when it was over, the useful items had been sold, but the non-useful items were gathered and put in trash bins for garbage pickup. So it will be at the end of the age. The angels will come out and separate the evil from the righteous and throw them into the furnace of fire, where there will be weeping and gnashing of teeth.

Again, the kingdom of heaven is like a flea market which displayed antiques in multiple rented spaces; before the market was closed, the good items remaining were gathered by the owners of the rented spaces, but what was left was gathered by the building's owner and thrown into huge dumpsters for garbage pickup. So it will be at the end of the age. The angels will come out and separate the evil from the righteous and throw them into the furnace of fire, where there will be weeping and gnashing of teeth.

Again, the kingdom of heaven is like a health inspector who visited all the restaurants in a town. At the end of the month, he posted his reviews. The restaurants following the city's codes were kept open, but those not following the city's code were closed. So it will be at the end of the age. The angels will come out and separate the evil from the righteous and throw them into the furnace of fire, where there will be weeping and gnashing of teeth.

Again, the kingdom of heaven is like a nut collector who used his nut gatherer to pick up black walnuts under the fruit-bearing trees; when it was full, he emptied it, sat down, and put the good walnuts into a burlap bag—to be sold to Hammons Black Walnuts in Stockton, Missouri—but threw out the bad. So it will be at the end of the age. The angels will come out and separate the evil from the righteous and throw them into the furnace of fire, where there will be weeping and gnashing of teeth.

Again, the kingdom of heaven is like a crab fisherman who lowered his cages into the ocean and left them there for several days; when each cage was full, he drew it into his boat, sat down, and, after wrapping the pinchers with a band, put the male crabs into a tank, later to be sold to the fish market, but the female crabs he returned to the sea. So it will be at the end of the age. The angels will come out and separate the evil from the righteous and throw them into the furnace of fire, where there will be weeping and gnashing of teeth.

Blind Leading the Blind

(Matt 15:10–20)

Jesus called the crowd to him and said to them, "Listen and understand; it is not what goes into the mouth that defiles a person's character, but it is what comes out of the mouth that defiles character." Then the disciples approached and said to him, "Do you know that the Protestants took offense when they heard what you said?" He answered, "Every plant that my heavenly Father has not planted will be uprooted. Let them alone; they are blind guides of the blind. And if one blind person guides another, both of them will fall into a pit."[5] But Peter said to him, "Explain this parable to us." Then he said, "Are you also still without understanding? Do you not see that whatever goes into the mouth enters the stomach, and goes out into the sewer? But what comes out of the mouth proceeds from the heart, and this is what defiles character. For out of the heart come evil intentions, murder, adultery, fornication, theft, false witness, slander. They are what defile a person's character, but to eat with unwashed hands does not defile character."

Jesus called the crowd to him and said to them, "Listen and understand; it is not what goes into the mouth that defiles a person's character, but it is what comes out of the mouth that defiles character." Then the disciples approached and said to him, "Do you know

---

5. Alternate Verses: (1) "Leave them alone; they are ignorant guides of the ignorant. And if one ignorant person guides another, both will remain ignorant." (2) "Leave them alone; they do not wish to learn the truth. And if a person who refuses to seek truth guides another to believe the same, they will both remain ignorant."

that the Catholics took offense when they heard what you said?" He answered, "Every plant that my heavenly Father has not planted will be uprooted. Let them alone; they are blind guides of the blind. "If one uneducated person teaches another, both will remain in ignorance." But Peter said to him, "Explain this parable to us." Then he said, "Are you also still without understanding? Do you not see that whatever goes into the mouth enters the stomach, and goes out into the sewer? But what comes out of the mouth proceeds from the thoughts of the heart, and this is what defiles character. For out of the heart come evil intentions, murder, adultery, fornication, theft, false witness, slander. They are what defile a person's character, but to eat with unwashed hands does not defile character."

Jesus called a crowd to him and said to them, "Listen and understand; it is not what one eats that defiles a person's character, but it is what comes out of the mouth that defiles character." Then the disciples approached and said to him, "Do you know that the non-Christians took offense when they heard what you said?" He answered, "Anything that my heavenly Father has not written will be erased. Let them alone; they are illiterate technology persons instructing others without online skills. And if one uneducated person teaches another, both will remain in ignorance." But Peter said to him, "Explain this parable to us." Then he said, "Are you also still without understanding? Do you not see that whatever one eats enters the stomach, and goes out into the sewer? But what comes out of the mouth proceeds from the thoughts of the heart, and this is what defiles character. For out of the heart come evil intentions, murder, adultery, fornication, theft, false witness, slander. They are what defile a person's character, but to eat with unwashed hands does not defile character."

Lost Sheep

(Matt 18:12–13)

Jesus asked his disciples, "What do you think? If a rancher has a hundred cattle, and one of them has gone astray, does he not leave the ninety-nine on the mountains and go in search of the one that went astray? And if he finds it, truly I tell you, he rejoices over it more than over the ninety-nine that never went astray."

Jesus asked his disciples, "What do you think? If a guide has a hundred campers, and one of them gets lost, does he not leave the ninety-nine on the mountains and go in search of the one who is lost? And if he finds him or her, truly I tell you, he rejoices over that camper more than over the ninety-nine who never left camp."

Jesus asked his disciples, "What do you think? If a swineherd has a hundred pigs, and one of them escapes, does he not leave the ninety-nine in the shed and go in search of the one that got away? And if he finds it, truly I tell you, he rejoices over it more than over the ninety-nine that never left the shed."

Jesus asked his disciples, "What do you think? If a dog breeder has a hundred puppies, and one of them escapes the kennel, does he not leave the ninety-nine whelps in the shelter and go in search of the one pup that escaped the puppy mill? And if he finds it, truly I tell you, he rejoices over it more than over the ninety-nine that never got away."

King Who Forgave Slave's Debt

(Matt 18:23–35)

The kingdom of heaven may be compared to a teacher who, preparing to post semester grades, wished to settle accounts with her students. When she began figuring grades, one student who had not worked with the group of students to which he was assigned and, consequently, had not submitted two of the three-page reflection papers, was summoned to her office, where he was told that he was going to fail her course. The student, sitting in a chair opposite the teacher, pleaded with her, saying, "Have patience with me, and I will turn in the two papers in a week; please give me an incomplete until then." And out of pity for him, the teacher of that student gave him a D and released him from having to hand in two papers.

But that same student, as he left the teacher's office, came upon one of his fellow students in the same class; and seizing him by the shirt collar, said, "You have my textbook; return it to me now so I can sell it." Then his fellow student pleaded with him, "Have patience with me, and I will return it to you." But he refused; then he went and had him arrested for stealing his textbook until he would return it. When his fellow students saw what had happened, they were greatly distressed, and they went and reported to their teacher all that had taken place.

Then the teacher summoned him and said to him, "You wicked student! I forgave you the two papers you owed me and gave you a passing grade because you pleaded with me. Should you not have had mercy on your fellow student, as I had mercy on you?" And in anger the teacher changed his grade to a F because he failed to turn in two required papers. So the heavenly Father will also do to every one of you, if you do not forgive your brother or sister from your heart.

The kingdom of heaven may be compared to a county collector of revenue who sent out the annual real estate and personal property tax statements. When she began the reckoning, one farmer who owed ten thousand dollars appeared before the collector of revenue and told her that he did not have the monetary resources to pay his taxes. She told him to sell the property and all the equipment on it, and payment could then be made. So the farmer pleaded with her, saying, "Have patience with me, and I will pay you everything." And out of pity for him, the county collector of revenue released him and forgave him the debt.

But that same farmer, as he left the collector's office, came upon one of his fellow farmers in the same county who owed him one final payment for a piece of equipment he had purchased; and seizing him by the shirt collar, said, "Pay what you owe me." Then his fellow farmer pleaded with him, "Have patience with me, and I will pay you." But he refused; then he went and repossessed the equipment until he would make the final payment. When other farmers in the area heard what had happened, they were greatly distressed, and they went and reported to the county collector of revenue all that had taken place.

Then the collector of revenue summoned him and said to him, "You wicked farmer! I forgave you both your personal property and real estate taxes because you pleaded with me. Should you not have had mercy on your fellow farmer, as I had mercy on you?" And in anger the collector of revenue reinstated his tax bill which would accumulate interest until he would pay his entire debt. So the heavenly Father will also do to every one of you, if you do not forgive your brother or sister from your heart.

The kingdom of heaven may be compared to the owner of a car dealership who wished to settle accounts with his debtors. When he began the reckoning, one debtor who owed five thousand dollars appeared before the owner; and, as he could not pay, the owner ordered his car to be repossessed. So, the debtor, standing before the dealer, pleaded with him, saying, "Have patience with me, and I will pay you everything." And out of pity for him, the car dealer released him and forgave him the debt.

But that same debtor, as he left the dealer's office, came upon one of his fellow debtors who owed him five hundred dollars for a car he had sold him; and seizing him by the shirt collar, said, "Pay what you owe me." Then his fellow debtor pleaded with him, "Have patience with me, and I will pay you." But he refused; then he went and repossessed the car until he would pay the debt. When other debtors saw what had happened, they were greatly distressed, and they went and reported to the owner of the dealership all that had taken place.

Then the dealership owner summoned him and said to him, "You wicked debtor! I forgave you all the debt because you pleaded with me. Should you not have had mercy on your fellow debtor, as I had mercy on you?" And in anger the dealership owner repossessed the car until he would pay his entire debt. So the heavenly Father will also do to every one of you, if you do not forgive your brother or sister from your heart.

The kingdom of heaven may be compared to an Internal Revenue Service (IRS) agent who wished to settle accounts with people who had not paid their income taxes for five years. When he began the reckoning, one person who owed seven thousand dollars appeared before the agent; and, as he could not pay, the agent ordered his house, car, and all his possessions to be sold, and payment to be made. So the person pleaded with him, saying, "Have patience with me, and I will pay everything." And out of pity for him, the IRS agent released him and forgave him the debt.

But that same person, as he left the agent's office, came upon one of his friends who owed him one hundred dollars for a loan; and seizing him by the shirt collar, said, "Pay what you owe me." Then his debtor pleaded with him, "Have patience with me, and I will pay you." But he refused; then he went and had his wages garnished until he would pay the debt. When other debtors saw what had happened, they were greatly distressed, and they went and reported to the IRS agent all that had taken place.

Then the IRS agent summoned him and said to him, "You wicked person! I forgave you all your back taxes because you pleaded with me. Should you not have had mercy on your fellow debtor, as I had mercy on you?" And in anger the IRS agent had him arrested, put him in jail, and ordered that his house, car, and all his possessions be sold in payment of his entire tax debt. So the heavenly Father will also do to every one of you, if you do not forgive your brother or sister from your heart.

The kingdom of heaven may be compared to a Sallie Mae Bank loan officer who wished to settle accounts with former students who had not paid their education loans. When he began the reckoning, one former student who owed twenty-one thousand dollars appeared before the loan office; and, as he could not pay, the loan officer ordered his car and all his possessions to be sold, and payment to be made. So the former student pleaded with him, saying, "Have patience with me, and I will pay everything." And out of pity for him, the Sallie Mae Bank loan officer released him and forgave him his debt.

But that same former student, as he left the loan officer's office, came upon one of his fellow former students who owed him five hundred dollars for a loan he had given him during their college days; and seizing him by the shirt collar, said, "Pay what you owe me." Then his fellow former student pleaded with him, "Have patience with me, and I will pay you." But he refused; then he took him to small claims court until he would pay the debt. When other fellow former students saw what had happened, they were greatly distressed, and they went and reported to the Sallie Mae Bank loan officer all that had taken place.

Then the loan officer summoned him and said to him, "You wicked former student! I forgave you all your loan because you pleaded with me. Should you not have had mercy on your fellow former student, as I had mercy on you?" And in anger the Sallie Mae Bank loan officer had him arrested, filed charges against him, brought him to trial, and convinced the judge to garnish his wages until he would pay his entire loan. So the heavenly Father will also do to every one of you, if you do not forgive your brother or sister from your heart.

Vineyard Landowner

(Matt 20:1–15)

The kingdom of heaven is like a tomato farmer who went out early in the morning to hire migrant laborers to harvest his crop. After agreeing with the migrant laborers for the usual daily wage, he sent them into his fields. When he went out about nine o'clock to pick up supplies, he saw others standing idle near the supply store; and he said to them, "You also go into the fields, and I will pay you whatever is right." So they went. When he went out again about noon to go eat lunch and about three o'clock to pick up the mail, he did the same. And about five o'clock he went out to get ready to close for the day and found others standing around; and he said to them, "Why are you standing here idle all day?" They said to him, "Because no one has hired us." He said to them, "You also go into the fields."

When evening came, the owner of the tomato farm said to the manager, "Call the migrant laborers and give them their pay, beginning with the last and then going to the first." When those hired about five o'clock came, each of them received the usual daily wage. Now when the first came, they thought they would receive more; but each of them also received the usual daily wage. And when they received it, they grumbled against the famer, saying, "These last worked only one hour and you have made them equal to us who have borne the burden of the day and the scorching heat." But he replied to one of them, "Friend, I am doing you no wrong; did you not agree with me for the usual daily wage? Take what belongs to you and go; I choose to give to this last the same as I give to you. Am I not allowed to do what I choose with what belongs to me? Or are you envious because I am generous?"

The kingdom of heaven is like a fish company owner who went out early in the morning to hire boats with crews to sail into the ocean and fish. After agreeing with the boat captains for the usual daily wage, he sent them out to the ocean. When he went out about nine o'clock to pick up supplies, he saw others standing idle along the docks; and he said to them, "You also go into the ocean and fish, and I will pay you whatever is right." So they went. When he went out again about noon to go eat lunch and about three o'clock to pick up the mail, he did the same. And about five o'clock he went out to get ready to complete the tally for the catch for the day and found others standing around the docks; and he said to them, "Why are you standing here idle all day?" They said to him, "Because no one has hired us." He said to them, "You also take your boat and go into the ocean to fish."

When evening came, the owner of the fish company said to the manager, "Call the boat captains and their crews and give them their pay for the fish they caught, beginning with the last and then going to the first." When those hired about five o'clock came, each of them received the usual daily wage. Now when the first came, they thought they would receive more; but each of them also received the usual daily wage. And when they received it, they grumbled against the owner, saying, "These last worked only one hour and you have made them equal to us who have spent all day on a boat in the turbulent sea with the hot sun beating on us." But he replied to one of them, "Friend, I am doing you no wrong; did you not agree with me for the usual daily wage? Take what belongs to you and go; I choose to give to this last the same as I give to you. Am I not allowed to do what I choose with what belongs to me? Or are you envious because I am generous?"

The kingdom of heaven is like the owner of a McDonalds Restaurant who began interviews early in the morning to hire people to work in his fast food place. After agreeing with the first group of interviewees for the minimum wage per hour, he sent them into the restaurant's kitchen. When he left his office about nine o'clock, he saw other applicants in the business; and he said to them, "You also go into the restaurant, and I will pay you whatever is right." So they went. When he left his office again about noon to go eat lunch and about three o'clock to pick up the mail, he did the same. And about five o'clock he went out and found others standing around; and he said to them, "Why are you standing here idle all day?" They said to him, "Because no one has hired us." He said to them, "You also go into the kitchen."

When evening came, the owner of the McDonalds said to the manager, "Call the newly hired employees and give them their pay, beginning with the last and then going to the first." When those hired about five o'clock came, each of them received a check for a full day's work at the minimum hourly wage. Now when the first came, they thought they would receive more; but each of them also received a check for a fully day's work at the minimum hourly wage. And when they received it, they grumbled against the owner, saying, "These last worked only one hour and you have made them equal to us who have worked all day cooking, serving, and cleaning." But he replied to one of them, "Friend, I am doing you no wrong; did you not agree with me for the usual minimum hourly wage? Take what belongs to you and go; I choose to give to this last the same as I give to you. Am I not allowed to do what I choose with what belongs to me? Or are you envious because I am generous?"

The kingdom of heaven is like an employer who wanted to hire someone to manage his business. After agreeing with the man with the high school diploma for the usual hourly minimum wage, he sent him to his office to begin work. Later, he met a woman with a bachelor's degree, and he said to her, "You also go into the office, and I will pay you whatever is right." So she went. He found another man with a master's degree, and the employer sent him to work in the office, too. Near the end of the day he noticed one other woman with a doctorate; and he said to her, "Why are you standing here idle all day?" She said to him, "Because no one has hired me." He said to her, "You also go into the office to work."

When evening came, the employer said to his account manager, "Call the four workers and give them their pay, beginning with the last and then going to the first." When the woman who was hired last came, she received the usual hourly minimum daily wage. Now when the first came, he thought he would receive more; but each of them also received the usual hourly minimum daily wage. And when he received it, he grumbled against the employer, saying, "This last woman worked only one hour and you have made her equal to us who have borne the burden of the day sifting through, sorting, and filing countless documents." But he replied to him, "Friend, I am doing you no wrong; did you not agree with me for the usual hourly minimum daily wage? Take what belongs to you and go; I choose to give to this last the same as I give to you. Am I not allowed to do what I choose with what belongs to me? Or are you envious because I am generous?"

The kingdom of heaven is like a superintendent of schools who needed to hire four new teachers. He interviewed many applicants and hired four to teach in the same school: one was just graduated from college; one had been teaching for five years; one had been teaching for ten years; and one had been teaching for twenty years.

When payday came, the superintendent told the principal of the school, "Call the teachers and give them their pay, beginning with the one who was just graduated from college and then going to the one who has twenty years of experience." The teacher just graduated from college received the usual district wage. Now when the teacher with twenty years of experience came, she thought she would receive more; but each of them also received the usual school district wage. And when they received it, they grumbled against the superintendent, saying, "This teacher is only recently out of school and you have made her equal to us who have been teaching for five, ten, and twenty years." But he replied to all of them, "Friends, I am doing you no wrong; did you not agree with me for the usual district wage? Take what belongs to you and go; I choose to give to this last the same as I give to you. Am I not allowed to do what I choose with what belongs to me? Or are you envious because I am generous?"

The kingdom of heaven is like a pool owner who went out at the beginning of summer to hire lifeguards for his pool. After signing a contract for the usual summer pay, he sent them to his pool. Going out the second month of summer he saw others standing around at the video arcade, and he said them, "You, too, go to my pool, and I will give you what is right." So they went after signing a contract for the usual summer's wage. The man went out again the next two weeks and did the same. Going out the last week of summer, he found others standing around and said to them, "Why do you stand around all day and do nothing?" They answered, "Because no one has hired us." He said to them, "You, too, go to my pool."

When it was the end of the summer, the owner of the pool said to his manager, "Call together the lifeguards and give them their pay, beginning with the last and ending with the first." When those who had started the last week of summer came, each received a check for the usual summer wage. So, when the first came, they thought that they would receive a check for more, but each of them also got the usual wage. On receiving it they complained to the pool owner saying, "These last ones worked only one week, and you have made them equal to us, who worked all summer in the heat." He said to them in reply, "My friends, I am not cheating you. Did you not agree with me and sign a contract for the usual summer wage? Take what is yours and go. What if I want to give these last ones the same as you? Am I not free to do as I want with my money? Are you envious because I am generous?"[6]

6. Toth, "Literature."

The kingdom of heaven is like the owner of a movie theater who went outside early in the morning to see patrons, who had begun to stand in line to buy tickets to see the latest Star Wars film. He went out about nine o'clock and saw that the line was getting longer. When he went out again about noon and about three o'clock in the afternoon in humid, 100-degree weather, he noted that the people in line would just about fill his theater. And about five o'clock he went out to count those in line before he opened the theater at six p.m. to sell tickets. However, the owner went to the back of the line where people had been waiting only five minutes, and he invited them to come into the cool, air-conditioned theater first to buy their tickets. Now when those who had been standing in line for the longest saw what was happening, they grumbled against the theater owner, saying, "These last stood in line for five minutes and you have made them equal to us who have stood in the scorching heat for over five hours." But he replied to one of them, "Friend, I am doing you no wrong; by standing in line did you not agree with me for the usual cost of a movie ticket? Either wait a little longer or go; I choose to sell to this last the same as I sell to you. Am I not allowed to do what I choose with the theater that belongs to me? Or are you envious because I am generous?"[7]

Two Sons

(Matt 21:28–31b)

Jesus said, "What do you think? A man had two sons; he sent to the first and said, 'Son, go work in the garage today and fix the flat tire on the truck.' He answered, 'I will not'; but later he changed his mind and went. The father went to the second and said the same; and he answered, 'I'll go, sir'; but he did not go. Which of the two did the will of his father?"

The bishops and the church elders said, "The first." Jesus said to them, "Truly I tell you, the drug addicts, the homeless, and the hookers are going into the kingdom of God ahead of you. For many

7. Adapted from Dreyer, "God only Knows," 41.

laity came to you in the way of righteousness and you did not believe them, but the drug addicts, the homeless, and the hookers believed them; and even after you saw it, you did not change your minds and believe them."

Jesus said, "What do you think? A woman had two daughters; she sent to the first and said, 'Daughter, go into the kitchen, do the dishes, and fix dinner.' She answered, 'I will not'; but later she changed her mind and went. The mother went to the second and said the same; and she answered, 'I'll go, mother'; but she did not go. Which of the two did the will of her mother?"

The priests and deacons said, "The first." Jesus said to them, "Truly I tell you, the drug addicts, the homeless, and the hookers are going into the kingdom of God ahead of you. For many laity came to you in the way of righteousness and you did not believe them, but the drug addicts, the homeless, and the hookers believed them; and even after you saw it, you did not change your minds and believe them."

Jesus said, "What do you think? A parent had two children; he sent to the elder and said, 'Go, clean your room.' He answered, 'I will not'; but later he changed his mind and went. The parent went to the younger and said the same; and she answered, 'I'll go'; but she did not go. Which of the two did the will of the parent?"

The other parent said, "The elder." Jesus said, "Truly I tell you, the thieves, the drug dealers, and the gang members are going into the kingdom of God ahead of you. For many parents came to you in the way of righteousness and you did not believe them, but the thieves, the drug addicts, and the gang members believed them; and even after you saw it, you did not change your minds and believe them."

Jesus said, "What do you think? A president had two cabinet members; he sent to one and said, 'Sir, go work on that new immigration bill.' He answered, 'I will not'; but later he changed his mind and went. The president went to the other cabinet member and said the same; and he answered, 'I'll go, Mr. President'; but he did not go. Which of the two did the will of the president?"

The senators said, "The first." Jesus said to them, "Truly I tell you, the lobbyists, protestors, and members of the opposite party are going into the kingdom of God ahead of you. For many government employees came to you in the way of righteousness and you did not believe them, but the lobbyists, protestors, and members of the opposite party believed them; and even after you saw it, you did not change your minds and believe them."

Jesus said, "What do you think? There was a young woman named Jenny who worked in a restaurant. One day she came down suddenly with a virus and had to call in sick at the last minute. Her manager was very understanding and, although he needed her in the restaurant, he let her stay home and rest without asking any questions. A few weeks later Jenny was asked out on a date by a young man she had been admiring for quite a while. She asked a friend of hers to work for her so she could go out on the date. Her friend agreed, and Jenny considered the matter to be settled. But the night of her date her friend came down with the flu and called Jenny, telling her how sorry she was that she could not work for her and to forgive her for not being able to take her place. Jenny, being so angry and disappointed, gave her friend a terrible time about it and ridiculed her repeatedly. She then decided that since her friend agreed to work, she would have to suffer the consequences of not being there and proceeded to go out on her date. The next day when her manager had heard the story, he became very angry and told Jenny that she no longer had a job working in the restaurant.[8]

Jesus said, "What do you think? A man had two daughters. He came to the first and said, 'Daughter, go into the kitchen and help your mother prepare dinner.' She said in reply, 'I will not,' but afterwards she changed her mind and went. The man came to the other daughter and gave the same order. She answered, 'Yes, I will,' but did not go. Which of the two did her father's will? The evangelists answered, 'The first.' Jesus said to them, 'Amen, I say to you, drug dealers and thieves are entering the kingdom of God before you. When preachers came to you in the way of righteousness,

8. McGinnis, "Literature."

you did not believe them, but drug dealers and thieves did. Yet even when you saw that, you did not later change your minds and believe him."[9]

Vineyard

(Matt 21:33–41)

Jesus began to speak to the religious authorities: "Listen to another parable. A man started a pre-owned car lot, put a fence around it, built a small office, and installed security and surveillance cameras; then he leased it to a manager and took a trip to Europe. At the end of the fiscal year, he sent his household servants to the manager to collect from him his share of the profits of the used car lot. But the manager seized the servants and beat one with a tire tool, killed another with a handgun, and pelted another with bricks. Again he sent other servants, more than the first; and he treated them in the same way. Finally he sent his son to the manager, saying, 'He will respect my son.' But when the manger saw the son, he said to himself, 'This is the heir; I will kill him, and the pre-owned car lot will be mine.' So he seized him, threw him out of the car lot, and killed him. Now when the owner of the used-car lot comes, what will he do to that manager?' They said to him, 'He will put that wretched manager to a miserable death, and lease the pre-owned car lot to another tenant who will give him his share of the profits at the end of the fiscal year.'

Jesus began to speak to the religious authorities: "Listen to another parable. There was a landowner in Hotchkiss, Colorado, who planted an apple orchard, put an eight-foot high fence around it to keep out the deer, dug mini-ditches to guide water from the main ditch to the trees, and installed security and surveillance cameras; then he leased it to a local farmer and took a trip to Europe. In October when harvest time had come, he sent his household servants to the farmer to collect from him his share of the profits of the orchard. But the farmer seized the servants and beat

9. Toth, "Literature."

one with a hoe handle, killed another with a pickaxe, and pelted another with large stones. Again he sent other servants, more than the first; and he treated them in the same way. Finally he sent his son to the farmer, saying, 'He will respect my son.' But when the farmer saw the son, he said to himself, 'This is the heir; I will kill him, and the orchard will be mine.' So he seized him, threw him out of the orchard, and killed him. Now when the owner of the orchard comes, what will he do to that farmer?' They said to him, 'He will put that wretched farmer to a miserable death, and lease the orchard to another tenant who will give him his share of the profits at harvest time.'

Jesus began to speak to the religious authorities: "Listen to another parable. Once upon a time there lived a very kind and noble real estate developer, who had a son named Mark, who came to him requesting a favor. He said to his father, 'Father, I have three friends who are out of work; could you give them jobs?' The father agreed, and the very next day put them in charge of three houses to maintain and watch over as landlords. But when the developer sent real estate agents to collect his portion of the rent the land-lords had collected, they threatened them and told them they were keeping the rent because they were not paid enough. The developer was shocked and again he sent his agents to collect the money the landlords owed him. Again they threatened his workers and kept the funds. Then the developer sent his son to reason with them in the hope that they would respect him. This time they did not even open the door to speak to him or dispute the matter. Finally, as a last resort, the developer called the police and had them evicted and put in jail. He then chose three people he felt would do as he wished and entrusted the care of the houses to them."[10]

Jesus began to speak to the religious authorities: "Listen to another parable. There was a church-planting pastor who built a church, painted its walls, grew its congregation, and even built a sprawling playground for the young children. Then, he leased the building to temporary leaders while he traveled to another coun-try for a mission. When the time came for the pastor to collect

10. McGinnis, "Literature."

his monthly salary, he sent his closest friends to go collect it for him. But the new leaders seized his friends and beat one, killed another, and tortured the other. Again, he sent more friends, and they treated then in the same way. Finally, he sent his son to them, saying, 'They will respect my son.' But when the leaders saw the son, they said to themselves, 'This is the heir; come, let us kill him and get his inheritance.' So, they seized him, threw him out of the church, and killed him. Now when the pastor returns, what will he do with those leaders? They said to him, 'He will throw those wretches out, and replace them with leaders who will give him his due at the end of the month.'"

Marriage Feast

(Matt 22:1–14)

Once more Jesus spoke to the bishops and priests in parables, saying: "The kingdom of heaven may be compared to a CEO of a large business who gave the annual Christmas banquet for his employees. He sent his managers to call the employees who had been invited to the banquet, but they would not come because they were on strike, walking a picket line in front of the business. Again he sent department heads, saying, 'Look, I have prepared the banquet; the caterer has the steaks and chicken breasts prepared, and all the side dishes are ready; come to the Christmas banquet.' But they made light of it and went away, one to his home and his family, another to do last minute Christmas shopping, while the rest remained on strike and verbally abused the department heads. The CEO was enraged. He sent pick slips to all the employees on strike, informing them at as of December 25, all of them were fired.

Then he said to his office staff, 'The Christmas banquet is ready, but those invited were not worthy. Go therefore to the main downtown streets and invite every homeless person you find to the Christmas banquet.' The office staff went out into the main downtown streets and gathered all the homeless they found, both good and bad; so the banquet hall was filled with guests.

But when the CEO came in to see the guests, he noticed a man there who did not have a tie on, and he said to him, 'Friend, how did you get in here without a tie?' And he was speechless. Then the CEO said to the office staff, 'Bind him hand and foot, and throw him out into the dark alley, where there will be weeping and gnashing of teeth.' For many are called, but few are chosen.'"

The kingdom of heaven is like a father who threw a birthday party for his son. He sent a text to all of his friends' homes personally inviting them to come to the party, but they refused to come. He then sent another text and said, 'I have prepared everything for the party; the cake has been made, everything is decorated, and all you have to do is participate in the party.' But they paid no attention and went off, one to his home and one to his business. The rest deleted the text. The father was enraged and sent the rest of his family to destroy the people who ignored his message and burned their homes.

Then he said to his relatives, 'The party is ready, but those invited were not worthy. Go therefore to town and invite to the party as many as you find.' And those relatives went out into the town and gathered all whom they found, both bad and good. So the back yard was filled with guests.

But when the father came in to greet the guests, he saw there a man who had no clothes. And he said to him, 'Friend, how did you get in here without a shirt on your back?' And he was speechless. Then the father said to his younger relatives, 'Bind him hand and foot and cast him into the back alley, where there will be weeping and gnashing of teeth.' For many are called, but few are chosen.'"

Ten Bridesmaids (Virgins)

(Matt 25:1–13)

The kingdom of heaven will be like this. Ten off duty Swiss guards took their flashlights to St. Peter Square to meet the new pope. Five of them were foolish, and five of them were wise. When the foolish took their flashlights, they took no extra batteries with them; but the wise took one pack of two extra batteries with their flashlights. As the election of the new pope was delayed, all the off duty Swiss Guard became drowsy, sat down, leaned against the wall, and fell asleep. But at midnight there was a shout, "Look! Habemus Papam! (We have a pope!) Come and meet him!" Then all ten off duty Swiss guards got up and turned on their flashlights, but the batteries in them had died. The foolish said to the wise, "Give us two of your batteries, for our flashlights have gone out." But the wise replied, "No! there will not be enough for you and for us; you had better go to the Quick Stop and by some for yourselves. And while they went to buy batteries, the new pope came onto the balcony of St. Peter Basilica, and those who were ready stood below the balcony, welcomed, and cheered the new pope. Then, the balcony door was shut. Later the other Swiss guards came also saying, "Your Holiness, open the door so we can see you." But he replied, "Truly I tell you, I do not know you." Keep awake therefore, for you know neither the day nor the hour.

The kingdom of heaven will be like this. Ten contestants took their songs to sing before a panel of judges. Five of them were foolish, and five of them were wise. When the foolish took their music with them, they did not rehearse the songs; but the wise did practice the songs. As the judges were delayed in making a decision about the contestants, all of them became drowsy and went back to their hotel rooms, where they fell asleep. But early the next morning in the hall they heard a shout, "Look! The judges are ready. Come and hear them. They want to hear the songs one more time." Then all ten of the contestants got up and hurried to the theater to hear the decision of the judges. The foolish said to the wise, "Help us practice our music." But the wise replied, "No! there will not be enough time for you and for us to practice; you had better go to the practice room and go over your songs there." And while they went to the practice room, the five who were ready went into the theater; then the doors were closed and locked. The contestants who were ready sang their songs for the judges, who announced the winner of the contest. Later the other contestants came also saying, "Judges, open the doors for us so we can sing our songs." But they replied, "Truly we tell you, we do not know you." Keep awake therefore, for you know neither the day nor the hour.

The kingdom of heaven will be like this. Ten people stood in a very long line to buy tickets for a concert. Five of them were foolish, and five of them were wise. When the foolish took their cell phones with them, they did not charge them before leaving home; but the wise charged their cell phones and brought the chargers with them. As the computers in the ticket office crashed, ticket sales paused while the computers were rebooted; finally, all ten people got close to the ticket booth. There was a shout from around the corner, "Look! We are almost there!" Then all ten people turned on their cell phones in order to access their bank accounts and credit cards, but the cell phones had died. The foolish said to the wise, "Let us use your chargers, for our cell phones have gone out." But the wise replied, "No! there will not be enough time for you and for us to recharge our phones; you had better go home and recharge them. And while they went home, those who were ready made it to the ticket booth, where they bought and paid for their concert tickets with their cell phones. Then, the ticket booth was closed. Later the other five people returned also saying, "Open the window so we can buy concert tickets." But the ticket sellers replied, "Truly we tell you, we have no concert tickets left." Keep awake therefore, for you know neither the day nor the hour.

The kingdom of heaven will be like this. Ten miners took their flashlights and went into the mine to meet their supervisor. Five of them were foolish and five were wise. The foolish ones, when taking their flashlights, brought no batteries with them, but the wise each brought an extra set of batteries for their lights. Since the supervisor was delayed due to a meeting with another miner, they all became drowsy and fell asleep. At midnight there was a cry, "The supervisor is here; come down to meet him." Then each miner woke up and turned on his light. The foolish ones said to the wise, "Give us some batteries for our lights are going out." But the wise ones replied, "No, for then there would not be enough for us and you; go to a merchant and buy your own batteries." While they went back to the surface to buy some, the supervisor came, and those who were ready went with him. Then the door to the mine was locked. Afterwards, the other miners came to the door begging for it to be opened, but the supervisor said, "Amen, I do not know you." Therefore, stay awake for you know neither the day nor the hour.

Talents

(Matt 25:14–30)

"The kingdom of heaven is as if a father, going on a year-long business trip, summoned his three sons and entrusted his money to them; to one he gave five thousand dollars, to another two thousand dollars, to another one thousand dollars, to each according to his ability. Then he left on his year-long business trip. The eldest son, who had received the five thousand dollars, invested the money in the stock market and doubled it. In the same way, the middle child, who had two thousand dollars, did the same. But the youngest son, the one who had received one thousand dollars, put his father's money in a shoe box under his bed, where he knew it would be safe.

After the year-long business trip was concluded, the father of those sons came home and settled accounts with them. Then the oldest son, who had received the five thousand dollars, came forward, bringing five thousand more, saying, 'Father, you handed over to me five thousand dollars; see, I have made five thousand more.' His father said to him, 'Well done, good and trustworthy son; you have been trustworthy in a few things, I will put you in charge of many things in my business; enter into the joy of your father.' And the son with the two thousand dollars also came forward, saying, 'Father, you handed over to me two thousand dollars; see, I have made two thousand more.' His father said to him, 'Well done, good and trustworthy son; you have been trustworthy in a few things, I will put in charge of many things in my business; enter into the joy of your father.'

Then the youngest son, who had received one thousand dollars, also came forward, saying, 'Father, I knew that you were a shrewd businessman, not taking financial risks, and charging lots of interest on debts owed to you; so I was afraid, and I went and put your money in a shoe box and hid it under my bed. Here you have what is yours.' But his father replied, 'You wicked and lazy son. You knew, did you, that I am a shrewd businessman, not taking financial risks, and charging lots of interest on debts owed to me? Then you ought to have invested my money in a savings account in the local bank, and on my return I would have received what was my own with interest. So take the one thousand dollars from him, and give to the son with the ten thousand dollars. For to all those who have, more will be given, and they will have an abundance; but from those who have nothing, even what they have will be taken away. As for this worthless son, throw him out of the house into the outer darkness, where there will be weeping and gnashing of teeth.'"

"The kingdom of heaven is as if a mother, going on a year-long business trip, summoned her three daughters and entrusted her money to them; to one she gave five thousand dollars, to another two thousand dollars, to another one thousand dollars, to each according to her ability. Then she left on her year-long business trip. The eldest daughter, who had received the five thousand dollars, invested the money in the stock market and doubled it. In the same way, the middle child, who had two thousand dollars, did the same. But the youngest daughter, the one who had received on thousand dollars, put her mother's money in a jewelry box in her closet, where she knew it would be safe.

After the year-long business trip was concluded, the mother of those daughters came home and settled accounts with them. Then the oldest daughter, who had received the five thousand dollars, came forward, bringing five thousand more, saying, 'Mother, you handed over to me five thousand dollars; see, I have made five thousand more.' Her mother said to her, 'Well done, good and trustworthy daughter; you have been trustworthy in a few things, I will put you in charge of many things in my business; enter into the joy of your mother.' And the daughter with the two thousand dollars also came forward, saying, 'Mother, you handed over to me two thousand collars; see, I have made two thousand more.' Her mother said to her, 'Well done, good and trustworthy daughter; you have been trustworthy in a few things, I will put in charge of many things in my business; enter into the joy of your mother.'

Then the youngest daughter, who had received one thousand dollars, also came forward, saying, 'Mother, I knew that you were a shrewd businesswoman, not taking financial risks, and charging lots of interest on debts owed to you; so I was afraid, and I went and put your money in a jewelry box and hid it in my closet. Here you have what is yours.' But her mother replied, 'You wicked and lazy daughter. You knew, did you, that I am a shrewd business-woman, not taking financial risks, and charging lots of interest on debts owed to me? Then you ought to have invested my money in a savings account in the local bank, and on my return I would have received what was my own with interest. So take the one thousand dollars from her, and give to the daughter with the ten thousand dollars. For to all those who have, more will be given, and they will have an abundance; but from those who have nothing, even what they have will be taken away. As for this worthless daughter, throw her out of the house into the outer darkness, where there will be weeping and gnashing of teeth.'"

"The kingdom of heaven is as when an executive, who is about to leave for a business trip, calls in his employees and entrusts his wealth to them. To one he gave $500,000, to another $200,000, and to a third $100,000—to each according to his ability. Then he went away. Immediately, the employee who received $500,000 invested it into the stock market and doubled his money. Likewise, the one given $200,000 doubled his money. But the man who received $100,000 dug a hole in the ground and buried his boss's money. After he returned from his trip, the boss returned to settle accounts with his employees. The employee given $500,000 said, 'Look, I have made another $500,000.' The boss said to him, 'Well done good and faithful employee, since you were faithful in such a small matter, I will give you great responsibility; come share in my joy.' He said the same to the employee who doubled his $200,000.

Then the one who had received $100,000 came forward and said, 'I knew you were a demanding person, so out of fear I went and buried your money. Here it is back.' His boss said to him in reply, 'You wicked and lazy employee! If you knew I was demanding then should you not have deposited my money in a bank so that I may have drawn interest upon my return? Now then, take your money and give it to the employee with a million dollars.' For to everyone who has, more will be given. But from one who has not, even what he has will be taken away. And throw this useless servant into the back alley where there will be weeping and gnashing of teeth.'"

Last Judgment

(Matt 25:31–46)

"When the Son of Man comes in his glory, and all the angels with him, then he will sit on the throne of his glory. All the nations will be gathered before him, and he will separate people one from another as an orchardist separates the premium, flawless apples from the small, flawed apples, and he will put the premium apples in crates for sale to the grocery store and the small apples in crates to be made into applesauce. Then the king will say to the workers at his right hand, 'Take these crates of premium apples, which have been blessed by God, to the truck headed for the grocery store.' The workers will say, 'How did you grow such luscious fruit?' And the king will answer them, 'God provided rain and sunshine, and I tilled the soil and fertilized the trees.' Then he will say to the workers at his left hand, 'Take these crates of small, flawed apples, which have not been blessed by God, to the truck headed for the applesauce plant.' Then those workers will say, 'How did you grow such small fruit?' Then he will answer them, 'Truly I tell you, God provided little rain and sunshine, and I failed to till the soil and to fertilize the trees.' These apples will be hauled away to become applesauce, but the premium apples will fetch a very good price for the grocery story."

"When the Son of Man comes in his glory, and all the angels with him, then he will sit on the throne of his glory. All the nations will be gathered before him, and he will separate people one from another as a launderer separates light-colored clothes from dark-colored clothes, and he will put the light-colored clothes at his right hand and the dark-colored clothes at the left. Then the king will say to those at his right hand, 'Come, you that are blessed by my Father, inherit the kingdom prepared for you from the foundation of the world; for I was hungry and you gave me food, I was thirsty and you gave me something to drink, I was a stranger and you welcomed me, I was naked and you gave me clothing, I was sick and you took care of me, I was in prison and you visited me.' Then the righteous will answer him, 'Lord, when was it that we saw you hungry and gave you food, or thirsty and gave you something to drink? And when was it that we saw you a stranger and welcomed you, or naked and gave you clothing? And when was it that we saw you sick or in prison and visited you?'And the king will answer them, 'Truly I tell you, just as you did it to one of the least of these who are members of my family, you did it to me.' Then he will say to those at his left hand, 'You that are accursed, depart from me into the eternal fire prepared for the devil and his angels; for I was hungry and you gave me no food, I was thirsty and you gave me nothing to drink, I was a stranger and you did not welcome me, naked and you did not give me clothing, sick and in prison and you did not visit me.' Then they also will answer, 'Lord, when was it that we saw you hungry or thirsty or a stranger or naked or sick or in prison, and did not take care of you?'" Then he will answer them, 'Truly I tell you, just as you did not do it to one of the least of these, you did not do it to me.' And these will go away into eternal punishment, but the righteous into eternal life."

"When the Son of Man comes in his glory, and all the angels with him, then he will sit on the throne of his glory. All the nations will be gathered before him, and he will separate people one from another as a bank teller separates twenty-dollar bills from one-dollar bills, and he will put the twenty-dollar bills at his right hand and the one-dollar bills at the left. Then the king will say to those at his right hand, 'Come, you that are blessed by my Father, inherit the kingdom prepared for you from the foundation of the world; for I was hungry and you gave me food, I was thirsty and you gave me something to drink, I was a stranger and you welcomed me, I was naked and you gave me clothing, I was sick and you took care of me, I was in prison and you visited me.' Then the righteous will answer him, 'Lord, when was it that we saw you hungry and gave you food, or thirsty and gave you something to drink? And when was it that we saw you a stranger and welcomed you, or naked and gave you clothing? And when was it that we saw you sick or in prison and visited you?' And the king will answer them, 'Truly I tell you, just as you did it to one of the least of these who are members of my family, you did it to me.' Then he will say to those at his left hand, 'You that are accursed, depart from me into the eternal fire prepared for the devil and his angels; for I was hungry and you gave me no food, I was thirsty and you gave me nothing to drink, I was a stranger and you did not welcome me, naked and you did not give me clothing, sick and in prison and you did not visit me.' Then they also will answer, 'Lord, when was it that we saw you hungry or thirsty or a stranger or naked or sick or in prison, and did not take care of you?" Then he will answer them, 'Truly I tell you, just as you did not do it to one of the least of these, you did not do it to me.' And these will go away into eternal punishment, but the righteous into eternal life."

"When the Son of Man comes in his glory, and all the angels with him, then he will sit on his glorious throne. Before him will be gathered all nations, and he will separate people from one another as a vintner separates spoiled grapes from the healthy grapes. And he will place the healthy grapes on his right, but the spoiled grapes on the left. Then the king will say to those on the right, 'Come, you who are blessed by my Father, inherit the kingdom prepared for you from the foundation of the world. For I was hungry and you gave me food, I was thirsty and you gave me drink, I was a stranger and you welcomed me, I was naked and you clothed me, I was sick and you visited me, I was in prison and you came to me.' Then the righteous will answer him saying, 'Lord, when did we see you hungry and feed you, or thirsty and give you drink? And when did we see you a stranger and welcome you, or naked and clothe you? And when did we see you sick or in prison and visit you?' And the King will answer them, 'Truly, I say to you, as you did it to one of the least of these my brothers, you did it to me.'

"Then he will say to those on his left, 'Depart from me, you cursed, into the eternal fire prepared for the devil and his angels. For I was hungry and you gave me no food, I was thirsty and you gave me no drink, I was a stranger and you did not welcome me, naked and you did not clothe me, sick and in prison and you did not visit me.' Then they will answer saying, 'Lord, when did we see you hungry or thirsty or a stranger or naked or sick or in prison, and did not minister to you?' Then he will answer them, saying, 'Truly, I say to you, as you did not do it to one of the least of these, you did not do it to me.' And these will go away into eternal punishment, but the righteous into eternal life."

"When the Son of Man comes in his glory, and all the angels with him, then he will sit on the throne of his glory. All the nations will be gathered before him, and he will separate people one from another as customs officials separate natives from immigrants, and he will put the natives in the line at his right hand and immigrants in the line at the left. Then the customs authority will say to those at his right hand, 'Come, you that are blessed by the Father, inherit the kingdom prepared for you from the foundation of the world; for I was hungry and you gave me food, I was thirsty and you gave me something to drink, I was a stranger and you welcomed me, I was naked and you gave me clothing, I was sick and you took care of me, I was in prison and you visited me.' Then the righteous will answer him, 'Lord, when was it that we saw you hungry and gave you food, or thirsty and gave you something to drink? And when was it that we saw you a stranger and welcomed you, or naked and gave you clothing? And when was it that we saw you sick or in prison and visited you?' And the customs authority will answer them, 'Truly I tell you, just as you did it to one of the least of these who are members of my family, you did it to me.' Then he will say to those at his left hand, 'You that are accursed, depart from me into the eternal fire prepared for the devil and his angels; for I was hungry and you gave me no food, I was thirsty and you gave me nothing to drink, I was a stranger and you did not welcome me, naked and you did not give me clothing, sick and in prison and you did not visit me.' Then they also will answer, 'Sir, when was it that we saw you hungry or thirsty or a stranger or naked or sick or in prison, and did not take care of you?" Then he will answer them, 'Truly I tell you, just as you did not do it to one of the least of these, you did not do it to me.' And these will go away into immigration services, but the righteous into their native country."

"When the Son of Man comes in his glory, and all the angels with him, then he will sit on the throne of his glory. All the nations will be gathered before him, and he will separate people one from another as a judge separates ordinary good citizens from crooks, thieves, drug addicts, murderers, and politicians, and he will put the ordinary good citizens at his right hand and the reprobate of society at the left. Then the judge will say to those at his right hand, 'Come, you that are blessed by my Father, inherit the kingdom prepared for you from the foundation of the world; for I was hungry and you gave me food, I was thirsty and you gave me something to drink, I was a stranger and you welcomed me, I was naked and you gave me clothing, I was sick and you took care of me, I was in prison and you visited me.' Then the righteous will answer him, 'Lord, when was it that we saw you hungry and gave you food, or thirsty and gave you something to drink? And when was it that we saw you a stranger and welcomed you, or naked and gave you clothing? And when was it that we saw you sick or in prison and visited you?' And the judge will answer them, 'Truly I tell you, just as you did it to one of the least of these who are members of my family, you did it to me.' Then he will say to those at his left hand, 'You that are accursed, depart from me into the eternal fire prepared for the devil and his angels; for I was hungry and you gave me no food, I was thirsty and you gave me nothing to drink, I was a stranger and you did not welcome me, naked and you did not give me clothing, sick and in prison and you did not visit me.' Then they also will answer, 'Judge, when was it that we saw you hungry or thirsty or a stranger or naked or sick or in prison, and did not take care of you?" Then he will answer them, 'Truly I tell you, just as you did not do it to one of the least of these, you did not do it to me.' And these will go away into eternal prison, but the righteous into eternal life."

2

Parables in Mark's Gospel

Patches and Wineskins

(Mark 2:21–22)

JESUS TOLD THOSE WHO had asked him about the lack of fasting of his disciples: "No one patches up a relationship by remembering bad feelings; otherwise, the bad feelings split the relationship, the old from the new beginning, and worse feelings occur. And no one puts a new relationship into an old friendship paradigm; otherwise, the new relationship will die and the friendship will be lost; but one begins a new relationship with a new paradigm."

Jesus told those who had asked him about the lack of fasting of his disciples: "No one patches a hole in a plaster wall and paints over it immediately; otherwise, the patch dries and shrinks and the paint peels off—the new from the old—and a worse hole is made in the wall. And no one puts a new patch over a good eye; otherwise, one will not be able to see properly and diminish the sight of the good eye, and so a patch is placed over a diseased or infected eye to protect it during healing."

Satan Cannot Cast out Satan

(Mark 3:23–27)

Jesus called the doctoral students, and spoke to them in parables: "How can a drug boss cast out drugs? If his territory is divided against itself, that territory cannot stand. And if a prostitution ring is divided against itself, that pimp will not be able to stand. And if alcohol has risen up against itself and is divided, it cannot stand, but prohibition has come. But no one can enter a house with ADT security and door bells that take pictures and rob it without first disarming all the security systems; then indeed the house can be robbed."

Jesus called the doctoral students, and spoke to them in parables: "How can the president impeach himself? If a country is divided against itself, that country cannot stand. And if a house is divided against itself, that house will not be able to stand. And if the president has risen up against himself and is divided, he cannot stand, but his end has come. But no one can enter a heavily armed man's house and steal his property without first tying up the heavily armed man; then indeed the house can be pillaged."

Sower and Seed

(Mark 4:3–9)

Listen! Snow began to fall on a mountain and its surrounding terrain. Some snow fell on the road leading to the mountain, but it melted immediately when it hit the asphalt. Other snow fell on the rocky base of the mountain, where it stuck very briefly, but disappeared as soon as the sunshine found it and melted into the desert-like landscape. Other snow fell below tree line, where slow melting occurred, watering the spruce and fir trees, which choked the undergrowth. Some snow fell onto the tundra, where it lasted for months, producing abundant flowers and grasses and forming flowing streams, and yielding thirty and sixty and a hundred gallons per hour. Let anyone with ears to hear listen!

Listen! A man started a fire in the circle of stones near his camp. And as it burned, tiny sparks few upward, but fizzled quickly. Other sparks fell on the ground, where the embers glowed for a short time before extinguishing themselves. Other sparks fell on a pile of leaves and set them on fire, but they quickly ran out of fuel and died. Other sparks fell among the evergreen trees, where they ignited a forest fire which burned thirty, sixty, and a hundred acres. Let anyone with ears to hear listen!

Listen! A hurricane began to form in the Atlantic Ocean. A few clouds began to gather and spin, but a front moved in and it collapsed at sea. Another hurricane began to form with wind speeds high enough that it was given a name. However, it quickly turned into a tropical depression. Another hurricane formed at sea, got a name, and was about to make landfall when a high pressure front pushed it away from land and back to sea, where it dissipated. Finally, a fourth hurricane formed at sea, grew in wind speed, and made landfall with gusts of wind that ripped off roofs and demolished structures while leaving one, two, or three feet of rain that flooded the area. Let anyone with ears to hear listen!

Listen! A tornado began to form on the high plains of Colorado. The clouds gathered, a watch was announced by the National Weather Service, but only rain fell and light winds blew. On the high plains of Kansas, another tornado formed as the dark clouds began to swirl and hail and rain fell and the winds blew hard; the tornado never touched down. In the middle of Kansas, a tornado funnel formed from the gray clouds and pounded the soil with hail and rain and mighty winds; it did little damage since it touched down for only a brief period in a wheat field. Closer to the Kansas-Missouri border a mighty tornado formed from black clouds with fierce winds and pounding rain. It touched down and swept over the land for miles destroying houses, barns, and silos in its path. Let anyone with ears to hear listen!

Lamp

(Mark 4:21–23)

Is a lamp installed under an opaque plastic tub or under one's bed and not on a table? For there is nothing hidden, except to be disclosed; nor is anything secret, except to come to light. Let anyone with ears to hear listen!

Does the sun rise only to set and to rise again? For there is nothing hidden, except to be disclosed; nor is anything secret, except to come to light. Let anyone with ears to hear listen!

Is an energy efficient light bulb placed in a fixture under a desk or under a table and not in a chandelier hanging from a ceiling? For there is nothing hidden, except to be disclosed; nor is anything secret, except to come to light. Let anyone with ears to hear listen!

Measure

(Mark 4:24–25)

Pay attention to what you hear; the measuring cup of kindness you give will be the measuring cup of kindness you get, and still more will be given you. For to those who have, more will be given; and from those who have no kindness, even what they have will be taken away.

Pay attention to what you hear; the measuring half of a cup of love you give will be the measuring half of a cup of love you get, and still more will be given you. For to those who have, more will be given; and from those who have no love, even what they have will be taken away.

Pay attention to what you hear; the measuring fourth of a cup of hospitality you give will be the measuring fourth of a cup of hospitality you get, and still more will be given you. For to those who have, more will be given; and from those who have no hospitality, even what they have will be taken away.

Pay attention to what you hear; the measuring third of a cup of peace you give will be the measuring third of a cup of peace you get, and still more will be given you. For to those who have, more will be given; and from those who have no peace, even what they have will be taken away.

Pay attention to what you hear; Price's square root law or Price's law pertains to the relationship between the literature on a subject and the number of authors in the subject area, stating that half of the publications come from the square root of all contributors. For to those who have, more will be given; and from those who have nothing, even what they have will be taken away.

Pay attention to what you hear; the home loan you get from the bank will be the home loan you give, and still more will you give. For to those who have, more will be given; and from those who have nothing, even what they have will be given away.

Scattered Seed

(Mark 4:26–29)

Jesus said, "The kingdom of God is like cactus in the desert. The wind blows the cactus seeds across the desert. Night and day whether the wind blows again or not, one or two of the million of seeds sprout and grow, though no one knows how. All by itself the desert sand produces first the sprout, then the stalk, then the flower, then self-pollination, then berries with seeds. As soon as the berries are ripe, the pods open and the winds pick up the seeds and scatter then far and wide."

Jesus said, "The kingdom of God is like parents with a newly conceived child. They sleep and rise night and day after the sperm fertilizes the egg. The body of the child grows in its mother's womb though the parents know not how. All by itself the fetus grows; first a zygote, then a blastocyst, then an embryo. The heart begins to pump blood; fingers and toes appear; the brain forms. As soon as the baby has matured, he or she is birthed for the time of labor has come."

Mustard Seed

(Mark 4:30–32)

Jesus said, "With what can we compare the kingdom of God, or what parable will we use for it? It is like an electron before the big bang, the smallest of all electro-magnetic particles; yet when it joins quarks, leptons, etc. it forms an atom and grows into an ever-expanding universe of solar systems, and puts forth stars, suns, and large planets, so that many different creatures can evolve and live on them."

Jesus said, "With what can we compare the kingdom of God, or what parable will we use for it? It is like a single cancer cell, which, when planted in a living organ becomes a living tumor that spreads throughout a body until it metastasizes many different organs."

Jesus said, "With what can we compare the kingdom of God, or what parable will we use for it? It is like a dandelion seed, which when sown in the garden is a small seed; yet when it is sown it grows up and becomes a great tree with large branches so that birds build nests in its shade."

Jesus said, "With what can we compare the kingdom of God, or what parable will we use for it? It is like a female frog, who lays eggs in a pond which are fertilized by a male frog. The eggs become tadpoles, which in turn become frogs, until the whole pond is overrun with them."

Jesus said, "With what can we compare the kingdom of God, or what parable will we use for it? It is like a magic grow capsule, which when placed in a cup of warm water is the size of any other capsule; yet it grows into an animal or other figure with which children can play, but if placed in a sink clogs the drain."

Jesus said, "With what can we compare the kingdom of God, or what parable will we use for it? It is like a cold front meeting a warm front; both are inconsequential until they meet over the ocean and create a hurricane, which puts forth a spinning mass of clouds a hundred miles in diameter and, in making landfall, brings destructive winds of seventy-four to 156 miles per hour."

Jesus said, "With what can we compare the kingdom of God, or what parable will we use for it? It is like a one-cent certificate of deposit at .02 percent compounded-monthly interest and a monthly contribution of five cents, yet over the course of thirty years it becomes $24.65.

Defilement

(Mark 7:14–15)

Jesus called the crowd and said to them, "Listen to me, all of you, and understand: there is nothing outside a person—no food, no drink, no thought, no sight, no hearing, no feeling, etc.—that by going in can defile, but the things that come out—rape, theft, murder, adultery, lying, envy, slander, pride, etc.—from within defile a person."

Vineyard

(Mark 12:1–9)

Jesus began to speak to the bishops, priests, and deacons: "A man started a junk yard, put a fence around it, built a small office, and installed security and surveillance cameras; then he leased it to a manager and took a trip to Europe. At the end of the fiscal year, he sent his personal assistant to the manager to collect from him his share of the profits of the junk yard. But the manager seized the personal assistant, and beat him, and sent him away empty-handed. And again he sent his personal mechanic to the manager; this one he beat over the head and insulted. Then he sent his grounds-keeper, and that one the manager killed. And so it was with many others; some he beat, and others he killed. He had still one other, a beloved son. Finally, he sent him to the manager, saying, 'He will respect my son.' But the manger said to himself, 'This is the heir; I will kill him, and the junk yard will be mine.' So, he seized him, killed him, and threw him out of the junk yard. What then will the owner of the junk yard do? He will come and destroy that manager and give the junk yard to another manager."

Then Jesus began to speak to the religious authorities in parables. "A man built an office building, put a security system in it, bought desks for computers, and painted the interior; then he leased it to another business as tenants and traveled to another country on another business venture. When the end of the following month came, he sent an assistant to collect his share of the rent. But the tenants seized him, and beat him, and sent him away empty-handed. And, again, he sent a repossession agent to take back the building; this one they beat over the head and insulted. He then sent another, and that one they killed. And so it was with many others; some they beat, others they killed. He had still one other, a beloved son. Finally, he sent him to them, saying, 'They will respect my son.' But those tenants said to one another, 'This is the heir; come, let us kill him, and the office building will be ours.' So, they seized him, killed him, and threw him out of the office building. What then will the owner of the office building do? He will come and evict the tenants himself and give the office building to others."

Watch

(Mark 13:33–37)

Jesus said, "Beware, keep alert, for you do not know when the time will come. It is like a man taking a trip to another country, when he leaves his home and puts his neighbors in charge, each with his or her responsibilities, and gives his front door key to one telling him or her to be on the watch. Therefore, keep awake—for you do not know when the owner of the house will come home, in the evening, or at midnight, or at dawn, or at midday, or else he may find you asleep when he comes suddenly. And what I say to you I say to all: Stay awake."

Jesus said, "Beware, keep alert, for you do not know when thief will come. It is like a man taking a trip to another country, when he leaves his home and puts his neighbor in charge and gives his front door key to her telling her to be on the watch for thieves. Therefore, keep awake—for you do not know when the burglar might come, in the evening, or at midnight, or at dawn, or at midday, or else he may find you asleep when he comes suddenly. And what I say to you I say to all: Stay awake."

Jesus said, "Beware, keep alert; for you do not know when the time will come. It is like a supervisor taking her lunch break, when she leaves the office and puts each employee in charge of his or her own work, commanding even the security guards to keep careful watch over the building in her absence. Therefore, keep awake—for you do not know when the supervisor will return, in ten minutes, thirty minutes, an hour, or two hours, or else she may find you slacking off and being lazy when she comes suddenly. And what I say to you I say to all: Stay awake."

Jesus said, "Beware, keep alert; for you do not know when the time will come. It is like a mother leaving the house to run errands, when she leaves home and puts her children in charge of doing chores, each with his or her own job, and commands the eldest child to keep watch over the rest. Therefore, keep awake—for you do not know when the mother will return, in ten minutes, in an hour, in two hours, or in three hours, or else she may find you playing video games, having accomplished nothing when she returns suddenly. And what I say to you I say to all: Stay awake."

3

Parables in Luke's Gospel

Patches and Wineskins

(Luke 5:36–39)

Jesus told the religious authorities and their staffs a parable: "No one takes a new piece of cloth and sews it as a patch on an old shirt or old pair of jeans; otherwise, the new cloth will be torn off in the wash, and the piece of new cloth will not match the old shirt or jeans."

Jesus told the religious authorities and their staffs a parable: "No one takes a piece of duct tape to fix a leaky pipe; otherwise, the duct tape will come loose, and the water will flow out of the hole in the pipe."

Jesus told the religious authorities and their staffs a parable: "No one takes an old rubber plug to fix a hole in a tire; otherwise, the plug will come out, and the tire will be flat."

Jesus told the religious authorities and their staffs a parable: "No one takes a new guitar and puts old strings on it; otherwise, the new guitar will not sound good and the strings will be broken.

New strings are stretched over the sound hole of a new guitar. And no one playing an old guitar desires a new one, but says, 'The old one sounds good.'"

Jesus told the religious authorities and their staffs a parable: "No one buys a new electric automobile engine and puts it in an antique, gasoline-fueled Model A Ford; otherwise the new engine will not fit and both the new engine and the Model A Ford will be destroyed. A new electric automobile engine must be put into the body of an electric car."

"And no one puts newly home-brewed beer into old bottles; otherwise the new beer will burst the bottles and will be spilled, and the bottles will be destroyed. But new beer must be put into new bottles. And, as is well known, no one after drinking old beer desires new beer, but says, 'The old is good.'"

"And no one puts new champagne into old bottles; otherwise the new bubbly will burst the bottles and will be spilled, and the bottles will be destroyed. But new champagne must be put into new bottles. And, as is well known, no one after drinking aged champagne desires new champagne, but says, 'The old is good.'"

"And no one puts new wine into new barrels; otherwise the new wine will not age well. But new wine must be put into old whiskey barrels. And, as is well known, no one after drinking aged wine desires new wine, but says, 'The old is good.'"

Jesus told the religious authorities and their staffs a parable: "No one buys a new gasoline-powered SUV in order to stop carbon emissions; otherwise, the new gasoline-powered SUV continues to add to carbon emissions. And no one puts new wine into used wine bottles; otherwise the new wine will be contaminated by the old bottles. New wine must be put into newly-made bottles. And, as is well known, no one after drinking well-aged wine desires new wine, but says, 'The old is good.'"

Jesus told the religious authorities and their staffs a parable: "No one builds a new coal-fired electric power plant in order to stop carbon emissions; otherwise, the new coal-fired plant continues to spew carbon into the atmosphere. And no one puts new port into used wine bottles; otherwise the new port will be contaminated by the sediment in the old bottles. New port must be put into newly-made bottles. And, as is well known, no one after drinking barrel-aged port desires new port, but says, 'The old is good.'"

Blind Leading the Blind

(Luke 6:39–42)

Jesus told his disciples a parable: "Can a blind person guide a blind person? Will not both wander into the busy street and get hit by a car? A college student is not above the professor, but everyone who is fully qualified will be like the professor. Why do you see the twig in your neighbor's yard, but do not notice the fallen tree in your own yard? Or how can you say to your neighbor, 'Friend, let me take out the twig in your yard,' when you yourself do not see the fallen tree in your own yard? You hypocrite, first take the fallen tree out of your own yard, and then you will see clearly to take the twig out of your neighbor's yard."

Jesus told his disciples a parable: "Can a person with severe allergies guide another person with severe allergies? Will not both with watery eyes wander off the sidewalk into the busy street and get hit by a car? A high school student is not above the instructor, but everyone who is fully qualified will be like the instructor. Why do you see the pollen in your neighbor's eye, but do not notice the pollen in your own eye? Or how can you say to your neighbor, 'Friend, let me wipe away the pollen from your eyes,' when you yourself do not see the pollen in your own eyes? You hypocrite, first take an allergy pill to remove the pollen from your eye, and then you will see clearly to remove the pollen out of your neighbor's eye."

Jesus told his disciples a parable: "Can a blind person on a movie set guide a blind person? Will not both wander onto the lot and get hit by a passing golf cart? A college student is not above his or her professor, but everyone who is fully qualified will be like the professor. Why do you see the false eyelash in your co-star's eye, but do not notice the fake eyelash in your own eye? Or how can you say to your co-star, 'Friend, let me take out the fake eyelash in your eye,' when you yourself do not see the false eyelash in your own eye? You hypocrite, first take the fake eyelash out of your own eye, and then you will see clearly to take the false eyelash out of your co-star's eye."

House Building

(Luke 6:47–49)

Jesus said: "I will show you what someone is like who comes to me, hears my words, and acts on them. That one is like a contractor building a new house, who, using a Caterpillar Excavator, dug deeply into the earth and poured the concrete foundation on rock; when a flood arose, the river burst its banks against that house but could not shake it, because it had been well built. But the one who hears and does not act is like a contractor who built a new house on concrete blocks placed on the ground without a foundation. When the river burst its banks against it, immediately it fell, and great was the ruin of that house."

Jesus said: "I will show you what someone is like who comes to me, hears my words, and acts on them. That one is like a contractor building a new house, who, using a Caterpillar Excavator, dug deeply into the earth, planted huge timber stilts, and poured concrete around them on rock; when a flood arose, the river burst its banks against the stilts that house was built on but could not shake it, because it had been well built. But the one who hears and does not act is like a contractor who built a new house on concrete blocks placed on the ground without a foundation. When the river burst its banks against it, immediately it fell, and great was the ruin of that house."

Jesus said: "I will show you what someone is like who comes to me, hears my words, and acts on them. That one is like a man digging a well for his family, who dug deeply until he reached an aquifer; when a drought came, dryness swept the land but this did not affect the family, because their well was *well* built! But the one who hears and does not act is like a man who dug a shallow well for his family. When the drought came, dryness swept the land, immediately their well dried up, and great was the ruin of that family."

Cancelled Debt

(Luke 7:41–42)

"A certain loan officer of a bank had two people with unpaid loans; one owed five thousand dollars, and the other five hundred dollars. When both filed bankruptcy claims, he cancelled the loans for both of them. Now which of them will love him more?"

"A certain person had two friends with unpaid loans; one owed five hundred dollars, and the other fifty dollars. When both were broke, he cancelled the debts for both of them. Now which of them will love him more?"

"A certain employer had two employees. One owed the company five thousand dollars, and the other owed five hundred dollars. When neither employee could pay his or her debt, the employer cancelled the debt of both. Now which of them will love him more?"

"A certain collegiate institution had two students. One student owed a tuition fee of fifteen thousand dollars and one student owed a tuition fee of three thousand dollars. When neither student could pay, as they were full-time students with no job, the dean cancelled the debt of both. Now which of them will love the dean more?"

Sower and Seed

(Luke 8:4–8)

"In autumn, a master gardener went out to a town's park to plant daffodil bulbs; and as he planted, some he planted near the trail, and they were trampled on, and the squirrels dug them and ate them. Some daffodils he planted in rocky soil; and as they grew in the spring, they withered for lack of moisture. Some he planted among thorny rose bushes, and the rose bushes grew with the daffodils and choked them. Some he planted into good, well-watered, and well-drained soil, and when they grew they blossomed profusely. Let anyone with ears to hear listen!"

"In autumn, a Kansas farmer went out to sow winter wheat; and as he sowed with his tractor, some seed fell on the road and was run over, and the birds of the air ate it. Some fell on the rocky soil; and as it grew it withered for lack of moisture. Some seed fell at the edges of the field among wild blackberry canes, and the canes grew with it and choked it. Some winter wheat seed fell into the good, tilled, fertilized, and furrowed soil, and when it grew, it produced a hundredfold for the spring harvest. Let anyone with ears to hear listen!"

"A butterfly refuge employee went out to release newly hatched butterflies into the wild. As the butterflies traveled, some landed in the desert; they were quickly scorched and eaten by birds. Some landed in the mountains where they were soon desecrated by the snowy conditions. Others landed in Missouri, where the weather was temperate for a few months allowing the butterflies to thrive for a short time, but the rapidly changing weather quickly wiped out any remaining butterflies. Other butterflies landed in California, a moderate climate that allowed the population to thrive and grow a hundred times greater in size. Let anyone with ears to hear listen!"

Lamp

(Luke 8:16)

"No one after turning on a flashlight while hiking at night covers the flashlight with his or her hands, nor does he or she put it in his or her backpack, but he or she shines it down the path so he or she may see what is up ahead."

"No one after cooking a meal for dinner hides the food under the table, or throws it in the trash, but puts it on the dinner table, so those who are dining may eat the meal."

"No one after planting a garden covers it with a tarp, or ceases to care for the plants, but he or she daily maintains the garden, so those who enter may enjoy the produce."

"No one after turning on an electric lamp hides it under a blanket, or puts it under a bed, but puts it on a table, so that those who enter a room may see the light."

"No one after turning on an electric ceiling light hides it with a canvas tarp, or hangs a drop cloth over it, but lets it shine, so that those who enter the room may see the light."

"No one after growing roses hides them under a barrel, or covers them with a plastic tarp, but lets their beauty be seen by all who pass by.

"No one after buying a rain gauge mounts it in the house, or in the garage, but puts it outside on a free-standing pole, so that the rain that falls into it can be measured."

Pay Attention

(Luke 8:18)

Jesus said: "Pay attention to how well you listen, for to those who have listened carefully, more understanding will be given; and from those who have not listened, even what they seemed to have understood will be taken away."

Jesus said: "Pay attention to how well you see, for to those who have seen the big picture, more insight will be given; and from those who have not seen even the noses on their faces, even what they seemed to have seen will be taken away."

Jesus said: "Pay attention to what you touch, for to those who feel things carefully, sensitivity will be given; and from those who have not recognized the smoothness and roughness of the earth, even what they seemed to have felt will be taken away."

Jesus said: "Pay attention to how well you listen; for to those who have great wealth, more will be given; and from those living in poverty, even what they seem to have will be taken away from them."

Jesus said: "Pay attention to how well you perceive; for the billionaires only will get richer; and the poor only will get poorer."

Good Samaritan

(Luke 10:30-35)

"A Republican woman was walking from capitol hill to the white house and fell into the hands of criminals, who stripped her, beat her, stole her briefcase, and went away leaving her half dead. Now by chance a Republican senator was walking down the sidewalk; and when he saw her, he passed by on the other side. Likewise, a Republican congresswoman came to the same place and saw her, but she had a meeting to attend, so she passed by on the other side. But a Democrat, while walking down the sidewalk, saw her and was moved with pity. He went to her and stopped her bleeding. He put the woman in his own car, brought her to a hospital, and took care of her. The next day he took out his credit card, gave it to the admissions desk, and said 'Take care of her; and when I come back, I will repay you whatever more you spend.'"

"A Democrat was walking from capitol hill to the white house and fell into the hands of criminals who stripped him, beat him, stole his briefcase, and went away leaving him half dead. Now by chance a Democratic senator was walking down the sidewalk; and when he saw him, he passed by the other side. Likewise, a Democratic congresswoman came to the same place and saw him but had a meeting to attend, so she passed by on the other side. But a Republican, while walking down the sidewalk, saw him and was moved with pity. He went to him and stopped his bleeding. He put the man in his own car, brought him to a hospital, and took care of him. The next day he took out his credit card, gave it to the admissions desk, and said 'Take care of him; and when I come back, I will repay you whatever more you spend.'"

"A white mayor was walking from his office to his home in El Paso, Texas, when he fell into the hands of criminals, who stripped him, beat him, stole his money, and went away leaving him half dead. Now by chance another white man was driving by; and when he saw him, he continued to drive. Likewise, a white woman was jogging nearby, and when she saw him, she continued her jog. But an illegal immigrant of Hispanic descent, while walking by, saw him and was moved with pity. He went to the mayor, stopped his bleeding. Then he put the mayor in his own vehicle, brought him to a hospital, and took care of him. The next day he took out all the cash he had, gave it to the admissions desk, and said 'Take care of him; and when I come back, I will repay you whatever more you spend.'"

"A black man was driving from Atlanta, Georgia, to Birmingham, Alabama, and after stopping at a motel, he fell into the hands of robbers, who stripped him of his Nike shoes, took his watch and wallet, beat him, and went away, leaving him half dead in his hotel room. Now by chance a white man, who was also staying at the same hotel, saw his door open and him lying on the floor, but he passed by not wanting to get involved. So likewise a white Baptist deacon, also spending the night in the same hotel, saw the door to his room open and him lying on the floor, but he had a meeting to get to and passed by. But a white, former Klu Klux Klansman, also staying at the same hotel, walked by his open door, saw him lying on the floor and, moved with pity, went into the room to see if he was OK. He called 911, and paramedics arrived to stitch his wounds and bandage them after cleaning them with antiseptic. The former KKK member went to the hotel's front desk and handed the manger his credit card, saying, 'Take care of him; and when I come back, I will repay you whatever more you spend.'"

"A displaced Iraqi woman was walking from Mosel to Baghdad, and fell into the hands of Iraqi Kurdish soldiers, who stripped her, beat her, raped her, and went away, leaving her half dead. Now by chance a Syrian soldier was going down the road; and when he saw her, he passed by on the other side of the road. Likewise, an Iraqi government official, when he came to the place and saw her, passed by on the other side of the road. But an ISIS soldier while traveling came near her; and when he saw her, he was moved with pity. He went to her and bandaged her wounds, using his own medical supplies to do so. Then, he found her burqa, put it on her, and helped her walk to the first house he could find. He told the owner of the house, 'Please take care of her.' He handed the man sixty thousand dinars, and said, 'Give her some food and a bed; and when I come back, I will repay you whatever more you spend.'"

"A gay man was marching in a Pride parade, and afterwards fell into the hands of straight robbers, who took his wallet, beat him, and went away leaving him half dead beside the sidewalk. Now by chance a fellow male marcher went by, saw him, and passed by. So, likewise a female marcher, when she came to the place and saw him, crossed the street and passed by. But a straight man, who hated gays, walked by him, and when he saw him, he was moved with pity. He went to him and raised him up, called 911, and held him until the ambulance arrived. He accompanied him to the ER at the closest hospital. Then he handed his credit card to the admissions officer, and said, 'Take care of him, and charge everything to this card. If you max it out, I'll repay whatever more you spend when I come back tomorrow.'"

"A local prostitute fell victim to a gang on a busy street corner. The members beat her until she was near death. The city mayor happened to be driving down the street while the beating was taking place, but when he saw the gang, he pretended to see something in the opposite direction. Also, a city judge drove by, and when he saw the gang, he ran the yellow light so as not to have to stop near the gang. But a black goat farmer who saw the beating was moved with compassion at the sight. He approached the gang with a big club and chased them off. He then poured water on the prostitute's wounds and bandaged them. He carried her to his truck and took her to the local hospital. That evening he wrote a check to cover the expenses and gave it to the hospital treasurer with the instruction, 'Take care of her. If this is not enough, I will repay you with I return.'"[1]

1. Toth, "Literature."

"A well-known leader of devil worshippers was in an automobile accident on his way from St. Louis to Chicago. The man was severely injured and in need of help. A Christian man driving by noticed the accident and stopped to help, but upon realizing who was involved in the accident, drove away without offering any aid to the man. A Christian woman then saw the accident and observed who the man was. She was moved with pity, and she saw to it that the man got to a hospital. On arrival at the hospital, she told the doctors to do whatever was needed, and that, if necessary, she would pay the bills."[2]

"During the recession of 2008, banks were foreclosing on homes nationwide, making thousands of families homeless. In Chicago, most of the people being evicted were diligent renters who had no knowledge that their landlords were delinquent with the banks. In Chicago's Cook County, law enforcement officers were schedule to evict residents affected by more than 4,700 foreclosures. This was when Cook County Sheriff Thomas Dart put a moratorium on all foreclosure evictions. Sheriff Dart couldn't support taking the law into his own hands, but, at the same time, he couldn't put innocent families in the street. Sheriff Dart said, 'It's one of the most gut-wrenching things we do, seeing little children put out on the street with their possessions. And the hard part is that these parents played by all the rules, and they're being traumatized.' In deciding not to evict these people, Sheriff Dart was using the power of his office compassionately rather than being blindly punitive. . . . Sheriff Dart reached a moral boundary he couldn't in good conscience cross."[3]

Friend at Midnight

(Luke 11:5–8)

Jesus said to the crowd: "Suppose you have a friend, and you go to his house at midnight, ring the door bell, awaken him, and shout,

2. Riddenhour, "Literature."
3. Adapted from Nepo, "Our Walk," 97.

'Friend, can you lend me a cup of flour, a cup of sugar, and a cup of milk; for a friend of mine has arrived, and I have nothing with which to prepare breakfast for him.' And he opens the upstairs window and answers, 'Do not bother me; the door is locked, and my wife and children are in bed asleep; I cannot get up and give you anything.' I tell you, even though he will not get up and give him anything because he is his friend, at least because of his persistence of ringing the door bell and knocking he will get up and give him whatever he needs."

Jesus said to the crowd: "Suppose you have a friend, and you call him at midnight, letting his phone ring and ring and leaving messages, and call him again and again until you awaken him and he answers the phone, saying, 'What do you want?' And you say, 'Friend, can you come to the county jail and bail me out? I got caught by the sheriff with illegal drugs in my car.' And he asks, 'How much is your bail?' He answers, 'Five grand.' He says, 'I don't have that kind of money. You need to call a member of your family. I and my wife and children are in bed. I can't get up and head off to the county jail.' I tell you, even though he will not get up and drive to the county jail to bail him out because he is his friend, at least because of his persistence he will get up and go and bail out his friend."

Jesus said to the crowd: "Suppose one of you has a friend, and you go to him at his workplace and say to him, 'Friend, lend me thirty dollars; for another friend of mine has arrived, and I have no money to welcome him with a meal.' And he answers from his office, 'Do not bother me; my office is closed to visitors, and my daily meetings have already begun; I cannot get up and give you anything.' I tell you, even though he will not get up and give him anything because he is his friend, at least because of his persistence he will get up and give him whatever he needs."

Rich Fool

(Luke 12:16–20)

Jesus told a parable: "The land of a rich man produced an abundance of wheat, corn, and soy beans. And he thought to himself, 'What should I do, for I have no place to store my crops?' Then, after thinking it over, he said, 'I will do this: I will add more and larger silos, and there I will store all my harvest and my goods. And I will say to myself, "Self, you have equity stored for many years; relax in your favorite chair, eat steak, drink fine wines, and throw parties."' But God said to him, 'You fool! This very night you will die of consumption. And all the stuff in your silos, whose will it be?'"

Jesus told a parable: "The stock of a rich man divided and divided and continued to make him lots of money. And he thought to himself, 'What should I do, for a stock crash or market correction is inevitable.' Then, after thinking it over, he said, 'I will do this: I will cash in all my shares of stock and put the money in the bank. I will say to myself, "Self, I have a retirement fund for the rest of my life; relax, drink fine wines, and travel around the world."' But God said to him, 'You fool! Tonight you will have a massive heart attack and die. And all the money in your bank account, whose will it be?'"

Jesus told a parable: "The stocks of a rich man produced abundant economic resources. And he thought to himself, 'What should I do, for I have reached the maximum balance allowed on my credit account and have no place to store the rest of my money?' Then he said, 'I will do this: I will withdraw all of my money from the stock market and put it into a large savings account, and there all of my money will be stored. And I will say to my soul, "Soul, you have ample financial resources not to have to work for many years; relax, eat, drink, be merry."' But God said to him, 'You fool! This very night you are going to die. And all of the money you have accumulated, whose will it be?'"

Waiting for the Master

(Luke 12:35–48)

Jesus said, "Ready! Set! Go! Be like children waiting for their parents to return home from a night out on the town. Blessed are those children whom their parents find alert when they come home; truly I tell you, they will dress them in their best clothes and have them sit down to eat, and they will come and serve them breakfast. If they come during the middle of the night, or near dawn, and find them so, blessed are those children.

But know this: If the owners of a richly furnished home had known at what time a thief was coming to break in, they would not have let their home be broken into. You also must be ready, for the Son of Man is coming at an unexpected hour."

Peter said, "Lord, are you telling this parable for us or for everyone?" And the Lord said, "Who then is the faithful and prudent manager whom his (her) boss will put in charge of his (her) employees, to give them their breaks at the proper time? Blessed is that employee whom his (her) boss will find at diligent work when he (she) arrives. Truly I tell you, he (she) will put that one in charge of greater responsibility. But if that employee says to himself (herself), 'My boss is delayed in coming,' and if he (she) begins to abuse verbally the other employees, men and women, and to drink alcoholic beverages on the job, the boss of that employee will come on a day when he (she) does not expect him (her) and at a time that he (she) does not know, and will reprimand him (her) severely, and fire him (her). That employee who knew what his (her) boss wanted, but did not prepare himself (herself) to do what was wanted, will be fired. But the one who did not know and deserved to be fired will receive a severe reprimand. From everyone to whom much has been given, much will be required; and from the one to whom much has been entrusted, even more will be demanded."

Jesus said, "Ready! Set! Go! Be like college students waiting for their professor to enter the classroom, so that they may be ready for class as soon as he comes. Blessed are those students whom the professor finds alert and ready to learn when he comes; truly I tell you, he (she) will turn on the overhead projector and load his (her) power point presentation, and he (she) will teach them. If he (she) comes at the beginning of the period or ten minutes late, and finds them so, blessed are the students in that class.

But know this: If a student in that class had known at what time the professor was coming, he (she) would not have shown up late to class. You also must be ready, for the Son of Man, the Divine Teacher, is coming at an unexpected time."

Peter said, "Lord, are you telling this parable for us or for everyone?" And the Lord said, "Who then is the faithful and prudent graduate student whom his (her) professor will put in charge of his (her) students on days he is away? Blessed is that student whom the professor will find researching in the library when he returns. Truly, I tell you, he (she) will put that student in charge of a small group. But if a student says to himself (herself), 'My professor is delayed,' and if he (she) begins to distract other students, men and women, to eat burgers and drink and get drunk, the professor of that student will come on a day he (she) does not expect him (her) and at a time he (she) does not know, and put him (her) with the D- students. That student who knew what his (her) professor wanted, but did not prepare himself (herself) by doing the necessary research, will receive a F for the class. But the one who did not know and did what deserved a F will receive a D+. From everyone to whom much has been given, much will be required; and from the one to whom much has been entrusted, even more will be demanded."

"Be dressed for action and have your phone set to ring; be like he who is waiting for his wife to return home from a business trip, so that he may open the door for her as soon as she returns and knocks on the door. Blessed is that spouse who is alert when his partner returns; truly I tell you, she will wash her hands and have him sit down to eat, and she will come and serve him. If she comes during the middle of the night, or near dawn, and finds him so, blessed is that spouse.

But know this: If the owner of the house had known at what hour the burglary was going to take place, he (she) would not have let the house be broken into. You must also be ready, for the Son of Man is coming at an unexpected hour."

Peter said, "Lord, are you telling this parable for us or for everyone?" And the Lord said, "Who then is the faithful babysitter of the businesswoman's children, to give them their allowance and meals at the proper time? Blessed is that babysitter whom the businesswoman will find hard at work when she arrives home. Truly I tell you, the babysitter will be put in charge of all her possessions. But if the sitter says to him(her)self, 'The parent is delayed in coming,' and he (she) begins to beat the children, get drunk, and neglect the children, the mother of the children will come home when the sitter does not expect and throw the sitter out into the street without pay. The sitter who knew what the mother wanted, but did not prepare him(her)self or do what was wanted will be thrown out into the street without pay. But the one who did not know and did what deserved the same consequence will receive pay, but still be thrown out into the streets. From everyone to whom much as been given, much will be required; and from the one to whom much as been entrusted, even more will be demanded."

Thief

(Luke 12:39–40)

Jesus said, "Know this: If the owner of the jewelry store had known at what time the burglar was coming, he would not have forgotten to turn on the security system. You also must be ready, for the Son of Man is coming at an unexpected hour."

Jesus said, "Know this: If the owner of a home had known at what time the parcel delivery truck driver was leaving a package on his front porch, he would have checked the video doorbell to see a thief taking the box. You also must be ready, for the Son of Man is coming at an unexpected hour."

Jesus said, "Know this: If the owner of the $400,000 house had known at what time the thief was coming, he would have called the police, who would have been waiting to catch the burglar. You also must be ready, for the Son of Man is coming at an unexpected hour."

Jesus said, "Know this: if the people of Indonesia knew that Krakatau was going to erupt, they would have escaped its deadly wake. You must also be ready, for the Son of Man is coming at an unexpected hour."

Jesus said, "Know this: if the people of Hiroshima knew that a nuclear bomb was going to be dropped, they would have evacuated the city. You must also be ready, for the Son of Man is coming at an unexpected hour."

Jesus said, "Know this: if you knew what time the car thief was coming, you wouldn't have let him break into your car. You also must be ready, for the Son of Man is coming at an unexpected hour."

Fig Tree

(Luke 13:6–9)

"A man had an apple tree planted in his vineyard; and he came looking for fruit on it and found none. So he said to the master gardener, 'See here! For three years I have come looking for fruit on this apple tree, and still I find none. Cut it down! Why should it be wasting the soil?' The master gardener replied, 'Sir, let it alone for one more year, until I hoe around it, put fertilizer on it, and irrigate it. If it bears fruit next year, well and good; but if not, you can cut it down.'"

"A woman living in Paonia, Colorado, had a sweet cherry tree planted in her vineyard along the North Fork of the Gunnison River; and she came looking for fruit on it on the Fourth of July, and found none. So she said to her vineyard manager, 'See here! For three years I have come looking for fruit on this cherry tree, and still I find none. Cut it down! Why should it be wasting the soil?' The manager replied, 'Ma'am, let it alone for one more year, until I hoe around it, put fertilizer on it, and irrigate it. If it bears fruit next year, well and good; but if not, you can cut it down.'"

"A business owner had a sales intern at his car dealership; and he came looking for an increased sales percentage from the intern but found that he hadn't sold any vehicles. So he said to the manager, 'See here! For three months I have been waiting for the intern to make his first sale, yet he has made none. Fire him! Why should we waste money on an unproductive intern?' The manager replied, 'Sir, let the intern work for one more month, allowing me to train him properly and develop his skills. If he becomes a great salesman, that's well and good; but if not, you can fire him.'"

"A man came home from work one day, and his wife met him at the front door. She was complaining about the old, broken down Ford Pinto that had been sitting in the driveway for three months. She wanted him to get rid of the car because it was cluttering the front of the house and keeping her from parking her car in the garage. He husband said to her, 'Give me one more month and I will have the car running again. If I don't have the car fixed in thirty days, I will have it towed away.'"[4]

Mustard Seed

(Luke 13:18–19)

"What is the kingdom of God like? And to what should I compare it. It is like a tiny chive bulb that someone took and planted in the garden; it grew and became a tree, and the birds of the air made nests in its branches."

"What is the kingdom of God like? And to what should I compare it. It is like a single horseradish plant that someone placed in the garden; it grew and became a tree, and the birds of the air made nests in its branches."

"What is the kingdom of God like? And to what should I compare it. It is like a rosemary seed that someone took and planted in

4. Ridenhour, "Literature."

the garden; it grew and became a tree, and the birds of the air made nests in its branches."

"What is the kingdom of God like? And to what should I compare it. It is like a tiny Princess Tree (*paulownia tomentosa*) seed that someone took and planted in the garden; it grew and became a tree, and the birds of the air made nests in its branches."

"What is the kingdom of God like? And to what should I compare it? It is like a bamboo seed that someone took and sowed in his yard. It grew, spread, and took over the entire yard, and the birds of the air made nests in its branches."

"What is the kingdom of God like? And to what should I compare it? It is like a single Zebra Mussel that someone placed in a lake; it multiplied, spread, and took over the entire lake, and the bottom feeding fish feasted on the waste."

"What is the kingdom of God like? And to what should I compare it. It is like an architect's single thought that inspired him to draw blue prints. From the blue prints a construction company built a tall skyscraper in which many people have offices."[5]

Leaven (Yeast)

(Luke 13:20–21)

Jesus said, "To what should I compare the kingdom of God? It is like radon gas, which cannot be seen, smelled, or tasted, but a home builder unaware let it enter three rooms in the basement of a new house until all the new tenants developed lung cancer (were poisoned)."

Jesus said, "To what should I compare the kingdom of God? It is like a third of a cup of salt that a female chef mixed in with three cups of soup until all of it was excessively salty."

Jesus said, "To what should I compare the kingdom of God? It is like a cup of baking powder and baking soda that a woman took and mixed with three gallons of bread dough until all of it was leavened."

5. Riddenhour, "Literature."

Jesus said, "To what should I compare the kingdom of God? It is like a cup of baking powder and baking soda that a woman took and mixed with three gallons of cake dough until all of it was leavened."

Jesus said, "To what should I compare the kingdom of God? It is like ground rat poison that a woman took and mixed in with the batter for three dozen sugar cookies until all of it was contaminated."

Jesus said, "To what should I compare the kingdom of God? It is like antifreeze that a woman took and mixed in with the drinks for her husband and two children until their kidneys failed and all of them died."

Jesus said, "To what should I compare the kingdom of God? It is like three invasive pythons that were introduced into the Everglades until the entire state of Florida was infested."

Jesus said, "To what should I compare the kingdom of God? It is like three European settlers in the United States who slowly introduced foreign diseases to Native Americans until the entire population was infected."

Jesus said, "To what should I compare the kingdom of God? It is like three Asian bighead carp, three silver carp, three black carp, and three grass carp introduced in the United States to clean algae from commercial fish farms and sewage treatment plants; through flooding they escaped to thrive everywhere in reservoirs, ponds, large rivers, and lakes."

Who Will be Saved?

(Luke 13:23–30)

"Someone asked Jesus, 'Lord, will only a few be saved?' He said, 'Strive to enter through the open window; for many church-going Christians, I tell you, will try to enter through the door and will not be able. When once the owner of the house has shut and locked the door, and you stand outside ringing the door bell and yelling, "Open the door, please," then in reply he will say, "I don't know you. Go away." Then you will say, "I ate and drank at your table, and you walked on my sidewalks." But he will say, "I don't know you; go away, you fraud." There will be weeping and shouting when you see Abraham and Isaac and Jacob and all the prophets in the kingdom of God, and you are outside. Then many non church-going people will come from east and west, from north and south, and will eat in the kingdom of God. Indeed, some Jews, Muslims, Hindus, Buddhists, Taoists, and others will be first, and some Christians will be last.'"

"Someone asked Jesus, 'Lord, will only a few be saved?' He said, 'Strive to enter through the pet door; for many, I tell you, will try to enter and will not be able. When once the owner of the house has shut and locked the front door, and you stand outside ringing the door bell, shouting, "Open the door," then from within he says, "I don't know you. Go away." Then you will say, "I shared dinner and conversation with you." But he will shout from within, "I don't know you; go away." There will be shouting and cursing when you see ancient Hebrew, Israelite, and Jewish patriarchs and prophets in the kingdom of God, and you are outside. Then many non-Christians of all kinds will come from all directions, and will enter the kingdom of God. Indeed, some who have been excluded by Christians will be first, and some Christians who consider themselves first will be last.'"

"Jesus went through one town and village after another, teaching as he made his way to Jerusalem. Someone asked him, 'Lord, will only a few be saved?' He said to them, 'Strive to enter through the closing bus door; for many, I tell you, will try to board the bus and will not be able. When once the bus driver has shut the door, and you begin to stand outside and knock at the door, saying, "Driver, open the door for us," then in reply he will say to you, "I cannot let you on, for you are not on my route." Then you will begin to say, "We have taken this bus many times before, we have tipped you well, and you have driven these streets for seven years." But the driver will say, "You never took time to introduce yourself, and I don't know where you come from; go away from me, all you latecomers!" There will be much anger and sadness when you see Abraham and Isaac and Jacob and all the prophets in the kingdom of God, and you yourselves thrown out. Then people from all over the city—east, west, north, and south—will come to the station and board the bus. Indeed, some are last who will be first, and some who are first will be last.'"

Behavior at a Wedding Banquet

(Luke 14:7–14)

"When Jesus noticed how the guests chose the places of honor, he told them a parable. 'When you are invited to a wedding reception, do not sit at the head table, because the wedding party is more distinguished than you; and the wedding planner may come and say to you, "This place is reserved for the members of the wedding party," and then in disgrace you would need to move to another table. When invited, go and sit at the table furthest away from the head table, so that when the wedding planner (the bride and groom) arrive(s), he (they) may say to you, "Friend, you have a place at the head table;" then you will be honored in the presence of all who sit at the head table with you. For all who think they are better than others will be humbled, and those who think of themselves as lesser than others will be exalted.'"

Jesus said also to the one who had invited him, "When you prepare a lunch or dinner, do not invite you friends, relatives, or neighbors, in case they invite you in return, and you will be repaid. When you prepare food, invite the street people, the disabled, and the diseased. And you will be blessed, because they cannot repay you, for you will be repaid at the resurrection of the righteous." (And you will be blessed, because they cannot replay you, for you will be repaid on the day of life for those who have done the right thing because it was the right thing to do.)

"When Jesus noticed how the guests chose the places of honor, he told them a parable. 'When you are invited by someone to a wedding ceremony, do not park in a place of honor that is closest to the door, in case someone who is more distinguished than you has been invited as well; and the person who invited both of you may come to you and say, "Give this person your parking place," and then in disgrace you would have to move your car to a parking place further away. But when you're invited, go and park in the place furthest from the door, so when the host comes, he may say, "Friend, move your car closer;" then you will be honored to park near the other distinguished guests. For all who exalt themselves will be humbled, and those who humble themselves will be exalted."

"He said also to the one who had invited him. 'When you offer someone a ride, do not invite your friends or brothers or your relatives or rich neighbors, in case they may invite you in return, and you would be repaid. But when you offer a ride, invite the poor, the crippled, the lame, and the blind. And you will blessed, because they cannot repay you, for you will be repaid at the resurrection of the righteous.'"

Great Dinner

(Luke 14:15–24)

"One of the dinner guests, said, 'Blessed is anyone who enters the kingdom of God.' Then Jesus said, 'Someone gave a backyard barbeque and invited many. At the time for the meal, he sent his son throughout the neighborhood to say to those who had been invited, "Come; for everything for the barbeque is ready now."

'But the neighbors all alike began to make excuses. The first said to him, "I have just closed on seventy acres of property, and I must go see it; please accept my regrets." Another said, "I have bought five new cars for my business, and I'm going to drive them; please accept my regrets." And another said, "I have just gotten married, and therefore I cannot come." So the son returned and repeated all this to his father.'

'Then the father, the owner of the house, became angry and said to his son, "Get on your bicycle at once and go out into the streets of our downtown and bring in the homeless, the disabled, and the diseased." And the son said, "Dad, what you ordered has been done, and there is still room in the backyard." Then the father said to the son, "Go out to the main streets and beg people to come, so that the backyard may be filled. For I tell you, none of those who were invited will taste my barbecued dinner.""""

"One of the dinner guests said to Jesus, 'Blessed is anyone who will eat bread in the kingdom of God!' Then Jesus said to him, 'A mother and daughter planned a family reunion and invited many. At the time for the dinner the mother asked her daughter to send a text to those who had been invited, saying, "Come, for everything is prepared now." But they all alike began to make excuses. The first said to her, "I am closing on a new seventy-acre home and property this evening; I can't make it, but maybe next time." Another said, "I have bought a new car and must pick it up this evening; I can't make it, but maybe next time." Another said, "I am coaching my child's baseball team tonight and can't make it, but maybe next time." So the daughter returned and reported this to her mother. Then the mother became angry and said to her daughter, "Go out into the streets and alleys around the house and bring in the poor, the crippled, the blind, and the lame." And the daughter said, "What you ordered has been done, yet there is still room." Then the mother said, "Go out into the outskirts of town and compel people to come in, so that my house may be filled. For I tell you, none of those who were invited will taste the dinner I prepared for them.""""

Salt

(Luke 14:34–35)

"Salt is good; but if salt has become insipid because it has sat around in a salt shaker for a long time, how can its saltiness be restored? It is fit neither for the garden nor to be poured into the toilet; they throw it out in the trash. Let anyone with ears to hear listen!"

"Salt is good; but if salt crystals have stuck together due to the humidity, how can it be restored? It is fit neither for the table or to be used in cooking; they throw it into the trash. Let anyone with ears to hear listen!"

"Motor oil is good; but once it is used, how can its viscosity be restored? It is fit neither for the car nor for the lawnmower; they recycle it. Let anyone with ears to hear listen!"

"Ever-ready, ordinary batteries are good; but once they are used, how can they be recharged? They are not fit to be used in any battery-operated thing; they are thrown into the trash or recycled. Let anyone with ears to hear listen!"

"Guitar strings make beautiful music; but if the strings are rusted or broken, how can they be restored? They are fit neither for an instrument nor to be recycled; they are thrown away."

"Meat is good; but if meat spoils from being left out of the refrigerator too long, how can its flavor be restored? It is neither fit for food nor for the trash can; it is thrown out."

"Glass goblets are useful; but if the glass falls to the floor and is shattered into a thousand pieces, how can the glass be restored? It is neither fit for drinking nor for the trash; it is swept up and thrown out."

Lost Sheep

(Luke 15:3–7)

"Which sheep herder, having a hundred sheep grazing in the high country of Colorado and losing one of them, does not leave the ninety-nine in the mountains and hike after the one that is lost until he finds it? When he has found it, he lays it on his shoulders and rejoices. And when he comes to his small camper, he calls together other shepherds in the area, saying to them, 'Rejoice with me, for I have found my sheep that was lost.' Just so, I tell you, there will be more joy in heaven over one sinner who repents than over ninety-nine people who did not stray and do not need to be found (who did the right thing and need no repentance)."

"Which Arkansas pig farmer, having a hundred pigs and losing one of them, does not leave the ninety-nine in the barn and go after the one that escaped until he finds it? When he has found it, he rejoices and guides it back to the barn. Then, he calls together his friends and neighbors, saying to them, 'Rejoice with me, for I have found my pig that was lost.' Just so, I tell you, there will be more joy in heaven over one sinner who repents than over ninety-nine people who did not stray and do not need to be found (who did the right thing and need no repentance)."

"Which rancher, having a hundred cattle and losing one of them, does not leave the ninety-nine in the pasture and go after the one that strayed until he finds it? When he has found it, he rejoices and leads it back to the field. Then, he calls together other cattle ranchers, saying to them, 'Rejoice with me, for I have found my cow that was lost.' Just so, I tell you, there will be more joy in heaven over one sinner who repents than over ninety-nine people who did not stray and do not need to be found (who did the right thing and need no repentance)."

"Which one of you, having one hundred children at a daycare and losing one of them, does not leave the ninety-nine children un-supervised and go after the one that is lost until he finds it? When he has found it, he picks up the child and rejoices. When he returns to the daycare, he calls together his friends and neighbors, saying to them, 'Rejoice with me, for I have the child that was lost.' Just so, I tell you, there will be more joy in heaven over one sinner who repents than over ninety-nine righteous persons who need no repentance."

The senior class at Sun Hill High School had always been commended on their scholastic achievement and their ability to work together, that is, except for Bill. Bill had been labeled as the rebellious, potential dropout since his freshman year, and un-til this point he had fulfilled everyone's expectations. Yet, when he went to tell the school counselor that he was dropping out of school, she did not let him leave for many hours. She sat and talked with him about his feelings and the things that were important to him until she convinced him to give the year one more try. She also made him agree to visit her in her office once a day. All the other faculty members spoke poorly about her ridiculous actions behind her back. They felt the school would be better off without the troublemaker. The counselor focused all her attention on Bill, for she knew that the other seniors were on the right track and could find their way without her guidance. Finally, graduation day came, and there was Bill along with the rest of the seniors waiting to receive his diploma. The counselor was so pleased and filled with satisfaction that she threw a graduation party for Bill. She knew that he would not have been there if it were not for all the special attention she gave him.[6]

Lost Coin

(Luke 15:8–10)

"What woman having ten national parks commemorative quarters, if she loses one of them, does not turn on the kitchen light, sweep the kitchen floor, and move the refrigerator, searching carefully through the dust until she finds it? When she has found it, she calls together her friends and neighbors, saying, 'Rejoice with me for I have found the commemorative quarter that I had lost.' Just so, I tell you, there is joy in the presence of the angels of God over one sinner who repents (who did the right thing)."

"What woman having ten diamonds in a necklace, if she loses one of them, does not turn on the bedroom light, sweep the floor, and move the bed and chest of drawers, searching carefully through the dust until she finds it? When she has found it, she calls together her friends and neighbors, saying, 'Rejoice with me for I have found the diamond that I had lost.' Just so, I tell you, there is joy in the presence of the angels of God over one sinner who repents (who did the right thing)."

"What woman having ten one-dollar bills, if she loses one of them, does not turn on the lights, sweep the house, and search carefully until she finds it? When she has found it, she calls together her friends and neighbors, saying, 'Rejoice with me, for I have found the dollar bill that I had lost.' Just so, I tell you, there is joy in the presence of the angels of God over one sinner who repents."

6. McGinnis, "Literature."

Lost (Prodigal) Son

(Luke 15:11–32)

"There was a wealthy businessman who had two sons. The younger of them on his sixteenth birthday, said to his wealthy father, 'Dad, give me the share of the inheritance that you have listed in your will after you have died.' So, he gave it to him. A few days later, the younger son gathered all he had, packed his car, and traveled to Mexico, and there he squandered his money in dissolute living on a beach in the Yucatan. When he had spent it all, a severe hurricane hit that beach, and he was in need. So he went inland and hired himself out to one of the Mexican citizens, who sent him to the barn to feed the pigs. He would gladly have filled himself with the slop that the pigs ate, but no one gave him even a bite of bread. But when he came to himself, he said, 'How many of my father's employees have food enough and to spare, but here I am dying of hunger. I will get up and go to my father, and I will say to him, "Dad, I have sinned against heaven and before you; I am no longer worthy to be called your son; treat me like one of your employees."'

"So he set off in his empty car, crossed the border, and went to his father. But while he was still far off, his father saw him coming down the driveway and was filled with compassion; after he got out of the car, his dad ran to him and hugged him tightly and kissed him. Then the son said to him, 'Dad, I have sinned against heaven and before you; I am not longer worthy to be called your son.' But his dad said to his household servants, 'Quickly, bring out my best cargo shorts and T-shirt and put them on him; put my gold ring on his finger and my new pair of Nikes on his feet. And get the best Omaha Angus steaks out of the freezer and thaw and grill them and let us eat and celebrate; for this son of mine was dead and is alive again; he was lost and is found!' And they began to celebrate poolside."

"Now his elder son was in the downtown office building working; and when he got home, as he pulled into the parking lot, he heard music and dancing poolside. He called one of his father's household servants and asked what was going on. He replied,

'Your brother has come home, and your father has grilled the best Omaha Angus steaks, because he has him back safe and sound.' Then he became angry and refused to go poolside. His father came out to the parking lot to plead with him. But he answered his father, 'Listen, old man! For all these years I have been going to the office every day and working my butt off for you, and I have never disobeyed or questioned any of your business decisions; yet you have never given me even a pork loin so that I might celebrate with my friends. But when this son of yours comes back, who has devoured your property with male prostitutes, you grilled the best Omaha Angus steaks for him!' Then the father said to him, 'Son, you are always with me, and all that is mine is yours, according to my will. But we had to celebrate and rejoice because this brother of yours was as good as dead and has come to life; he was lost and has been found.'"

"There was a wealthy businesswoman who had two daughters. The younger of them on her sixteenth birthday, said to her wealthy mother, 'Mom, give me the share of the inheritance that you have listed in your will after you have died.' So, she gave it to her. A few days later, the younger daughter gathered all she had, packed her car, and traveled to Mexico, and there she squandered her money in dissolute living on a beach in the Yucatan. When she had spent it all, a severe hurricane hit that beach, and she was in need. So she went inland and hired herself out to one the Mexican citizens, who sent her to the bar to make and serve drinks to the patrons. She would gladly have filled herself with the bar food that the patrons ate, but no one gave her even a taco. But when she came to herself, she said, 'How many of my mother's employees have food enough and to spare, but here I am dying of hunger. I will get up and go to my mother, and I will say to her, "Mom, I have sinned against heaven and before you; I am no longer worthy to be called your daughter; treat me like one of your employees."'

"So she set off in her empty car, crossed the border, and went to her mother. But while she was still far off, her mother saw her coming down the driveway and was filled with compassion; after she got out of the car, her mother ran to her and hugged her tightly and kissed her. Then, the daughter said to her, 'Mom, I have sinned against heaven and before you; I am not longer worthy to be called your daughter.' But her mother said to her household servants, 'Quickly, bring out my best pants and blouse and put them on her; put my gold ring on her finger and my new pair of Nikes on her feet. And get the best Omaha Angus steaks out of the freezer and thaw and grill them and let us eat and celebrate; for this daughter of mine was dead and is alive again; she was lost and is found!' And they began to celebrate poolside."

"Now her elder sister was in the downtown office building working; and when she got home, as she pulled into the parking lot, she heard music and dancing poolside. She called one of her mother's household servants and asked what was going on. She replied, 'Your sister has come home, and your mother has grilled the best Omaha Angus steaks, because she has her back safe and sound.' Then she became angry and refused to go poolside. Her mother came out to the parking lot to plead with her. But she answered her mother, 'Listen, old woman! For all these years I have been going to the office every day and working my butt off for you, and I have never disobeyed or questioned any of your business decisions; yet you have never given me even a freshly caught salmon so that I might celebrate with my friends. But when this daughter of yours comes back, who has devoured your property with female prostitutes, you grilled the best Omaha Angus steaks for her!' Then the mother said to her, 'Daughter, you are always with me, and all that is mine is yours, according to my will. But we had to celebrate and rejoice because this sister of yours was as good as dead and has come to life; she was lost and has been found.'"

"There was a record label agent who had signed two major bands on a tour. The more famous band leader said to the agent, 'Give us our share of the royalties that belong to us.' The agent then divided up the profits between them and gave them all of the royalties that belonged to them. A few days later the band stopped the tour short, packed their gear, and headed back home where they partied and squandered their royalty money. When they had spent all of their money, a great recession came over the economy and the band fell into poverty. So the band members went to a local business owner for help and he sent them to wash dishes at one of his restaurants. They would have gladly filled themselves by eating the leftover food on plates, yet no one spared them anything."

"Then the band members came to a realization and said, 'How many janitors at the record label office have food enough to spare, but we are dying here of starvation! We should get up and go to the record label office and say to our agent, "We have broken our contract and cost you thousands of dollars, and we are no longer worthy to be a band on your label; hire us as janitors." So, they set off and drove back to their agent's office. But while they were still in the parking lot, the agent saw them and was filled with compassion; he ran and put his arms around them and kissed them. They said to the agent, "We have cost you thousands of dollars and broken our contract." But the agent said to his other employees, "Quickly! Bring out fresh clothes, the best we have, and put them on them. Then go get the finest instruments from the studio and present the instruments to them as gifts so that they may make music again and we will celebrate their return; for this prized band was dead, and is alive again; the members were lost and now they are found." And they began to celebrate.'"

"Now the other less-famous band was just outside the studio, and when they approached the building they heard music and dancing. They called to an employee and asked what was going on. She replied, 'The other band has returned to the label, and your agent has given them the finest instruments in celebration of their return.' The lesser band became angry and refused to celebrate, even as the agent pleaded with them to come into the studio. But they answered the agent and said, 'Listen! For years we have done everything you have commanded. We have toured, recorded, let you keep our royalties, and lost time away from our families for you; yet you have never given us even a small allowance to go celebrate our own successes. But when this other band comes back, the one who has spent all of your money on prostitutes, and devoured your profits, you give them fine instruments.' The agent then told the band members, 'You are always with me, and all that is mine is yours. But we have to celebrate and rejoice, because this partnering band of yours was dead and has come to life; they were lost and have been found.'"

Dishonest Manager

(Luke 16:1–8)

Jesus said to his disciples, "There was a rich man who owned a chain of McDonalds Restaurants who had a store manager, and charges were brought to him that this man was skimming money off of the business. So he summoned him to his office and said to him, 'What's this that I hear about you? Give me a detailed accounting of your management of my store, because you cannot be my store manager any longer.' Then the manager said to himself, 'What will I do, now that my boss is taking the position away from me? I am not strong enough to dig ditches for construction projects, and I am ashamed to stand on street corners to beg. I have decided what to do so that, when I am fired as manager, people may welcome me into their homes.' So summoning his boss's debtors one by one, he asked the first, 'How much do you owe my boss?' He answered, 'A hundred bottles of cooking oil.' He said to him, 'Take your invoice, sit down quickly, and make it fifty.' Then he asked another, 'And how much do you owe?' He replied, 'A hundred pounds of wheat flour.' He said to him, 'Take your invoice and make it eighty.' And his boss commended the dishonest manager because he had acted shrewdly; for the people of this capitalist age are more shrewd in dealing with their own generation than are the Sunday, church-going folks."

Jesus said to the disciples, "There was a billionaire who had an accountant, and charges were brought to him that the accountant was embezzling his money and squandering his wealth. So, he summoned the accountant and said, 'Give me all of your records, as you cannot be in charge of my money any longer.' Then the accountant said to himself, 'What will I do now that I have been fired? I am not strong enough for manual labor, and I have no other technical skills. I have decided what to do so that my former colleagues may welcome me as an equal.' So summoning the billionaire's debtors one by one, he asked the first, 'How much do you owe?' And he said one hundred thousand dollars. He said to him, 'Quickly, sit down and make your bill for fifty thousand dollars.' Then he asked another the same question. He replied, 'One hundred shares of the company's stock.' He said, 'Take your outstanding bill and make it eighty shares.' And the master commended the dishonest accountant because he had acted cleverly."

Rich Man and Lazarus

(Luke 16:19–31)

There was a rich oil man, who was dressed in the latest Armani suits with fine white linen shirts and who ate caviar every day as he drank one-hundred-year-old scotch. And at the remote-controlled iron gate to his house lay a poor homeless man named Jim, covered with sores, who longed to satisfy his hunger with the cracker crumbs that fell from the rich man's table; even the wild dogs would come and lick his sores. The poor homeless man died and was carried away by angels to be with Abraham. The rich oil man also died and was buried in one of his Armani suits in a marble tomb in the cemetery. In Hell, where he was being tormented, he looked up and saw Abraham far away with Jim by his side. He called out, "Father Abraham, have mercy on me, and send Jim to dip the tip of his finger in scotch and cool my tongue; for I am in agony in these flames." But Abraham said, "Rich oil man, remember that during your lifetime you received your good things, and Jim in like manner evil things; but now he is comforted here, and you are in agony. Besides all this, between you and us a great canyon has been fixed, so that those who might want to pass from here to you cannot do so, and no one can cross from there to us." He said, "Then, father, I beg you to send him to my father's house—for I have five brothers—that he may warn them, so that they will not also come into this place of torment." Abraham replied, "They have Moses and countless prophets from world religions; they should listen to them." He said, "No, father Abraham; but if someone goes to them from the dead, they will repent." He said to him, "If they do not listen to Moses and the countless prophets from world religions, neither will they be convinced even if someone rises from the dead."

There was a rich man who lived at the top of a tower, was dressed in the finest designer clothing, and who feasted endlessly every day. And at the bottom of his tower lay a poor man named Pete, dying of AIDS, who longed to fill his stomach with what fell from the rich man's table; even the dogs would come and lick his sores. The poor man eventually died and was carried away by the angels. The rich man also died and was eventually buried. In Hades, where he was being tormented, he looked up and saw Pete watching peacefully. He called out to Pete saying, "Have mercy on me! Please, dip the tip of your finger in water and cool my tongue; for I am in agony in these flames." But Pete said, "Remember that during your lifetime you received your good things, and I in like manner evil things; but now I am comforted here, and you are in agony. Besides all this, between you and me a great chasm has been fixed, so that those who might want to pass from here to there cannot do so, and none can cross from there to us." He said, "Then I beg you to go warn my five brothers, that they may not also come to this place of torment." He replied, "They have Moses, Jesus, Bob Dylan, and all the prophets; they should listen to them." The rich man replied, "No! If someone goes to them from the dead, they will all repent." He replied, "If they do not listen to Moses, Jesus, Bob Dylan, or any of the prophets, neither will they be convinced even if someone rises from the dead."

Widow and Judge

(Luke 18:2–6)

Jesus said, "In a certain city there was a small-claims-court judge who neither went to church nor respected any other person. In that same city there was a homeless woman who kept coming to his courtroom and saying, 'Grant me justice against the man who took my house because I was not able to make the mortgage payments.' For a while he refused, thinking that she was just a nuisance; but later he said to himself, 'Though I don't go to church and I respect no one, yet because this homeless woman keeps bothering me by coming into my courtroom, I will grant her justice, so that she may not wear out my patience by her continued presence (reach over the bench and slap my face).' And the Lord said, 'Listen to what the small-claims-court judge says.'"

Jesus said, "In a certain city there was a technology business owner who was an atheist with little respect for any human being. One of his employees was a smart woman who kept coming to his office and saying, 'I am next in line for the position that just opened in this company.' For a while he refused to advance her; but later he said to himself, 'Though I don't believe in God nor do I respect anyone who works for me, I will give her the position, so that she does not file a sex discrimination case against me and my company.' And the Lord said, 'Listen to what the technology business owner says.'"

Jesus said, "In a certain city there was a coffee shop owner who was an atheist with little respect for any human being. One of his employees was a black man who kept coming to his office and saying, 'I am next in line for the manager's position that just opened in your company.' For a while he refused to give him the position because he was black; but later he said to himself, 'Though I don't believe in God nor do I respect anyone who works for me, I will give him the position, so that he does not file a race discrimination case against me and my company.' And the Lord said, 'Listen to what the coffee shop owner says.'"

Jesus said, "There was a president of a certain university who neither feared God nor respected any human being. And a student in that university used to come to him and say, 'Render a just decision for me against my teacher.' For a long time the president was unwilling, but eventually thought, 'While it is true that I neither fear God nor respect any human being, because this student keeps bothering me I shall deliver a just decision for her lest she finally come and get me fired.' The Lord said, 'Pay attention to what the dishonest president says.'"

"A poor woman, bruised and in pain, sat beside the road with food stamps in her hand. And it came to pass that a Cadillac stopped and a rich man with bright diamond rings on his fingers got out of the car and grabbed the food stamps. The rich man said to the poor woman, 'This is for your own good. You are lazy. Why don't you get a job?' And the rich man slapped the poor woman and said, 'That is so you will not forget this lesson!' Then the rich man hurried away to cash his Social Security check and to see about his subsidy for overseas advertising. As he drove away, the poor woman looked up and saw a bumper sticker on the Cadillac. It stated, 'Honk if you love Jesus.'"[7]

"In a certain city there was a lawyer who neither feared God nor had any respect for people. In that city, there was a woman that was the victim of a rape who kept coming to him and saying, 'Help me win my case, though I have very little money to give' For a while he refused; but later he said to himself, 'Though I have no respect for God or people, I will help this woman fight her case because she won't shut-up.' And the Lord said, 'Listen to what the unjust lawyer says.'"

Two Pray-ers

(Luke 18:10–14)

Jesus told this parable: "Two men went into a church to pray, one a Catholic and the other a Protestant. The Catholic, standing by himself, was praying thus, 'God, I thank you that I am not like other people: thieves, liars, adulterers, or even like this Protestant. I fast and abstain according to Church teaching; I give a tenth of all my income to charity.' But the Protestant, standing far off, would not even look up, but was kneeling and beating his breast and saying, 'God, be merciful to me, a sinner!' I tell you, the Protestant went home justified rather than the Catholic."

7. "Etcetera: Parable Update," 34.

Jesus told this parable: "Two women went into a church to pray, one a Catholic and the other a Protestant. The Catholic, standing by herself, was praying thus, 'God, I thank you that I am not like other people: spending money on makeup, taking birth-control pills, sleeping around, or even like this Protestant. I fast and abstain according to Church teaching; I give a tenth of all my income to charity.' But the Protestant, standing far off, would not even look up, but was kneeling and beating her breast and saying, 'God, be merciful to me, a sinner!' I tell you, the Protestant went home justified rather than the Catholic."

Jesus told this parable: "Two young men went into a church to pray, one a Christian and the other a Buddhist. The Christian, standing by himself, was praying thus, 'God, I thank you that I am not like other people. I'm damn good. I don't smoke marijuana, drink alcohol, or engage in sex with others. I volunteer at homeless shelters, and I make contributions to charity.' But the Buddhist, standing far off, would not even look up, but was sitting in the lotus position on the floor, beating his breast and saying, 'Great Buddha, through my meditation, fill me with wisdom!' I tell you, the Buddhist went home justified rather than the Christian."

Jesus told this parable: "Two men went to church to pray. One of the men was a deacon of the church, and the other was an ex-convict, who had spent many years in prison for robbing homes. The deacon went to the front row of the church and began to pray to himself, saying, 'God, I thank you that I am not corrupt like the rest of the world, such as this criminal across the room. I come to church every Sunday and Wednesday night, and always make a generous offering.' The criminal was in the corner at the back of the church. With his head bowed, he prayed, 'God, please be merciful to me, for I am a sinner.' I tell you, the criminal went home justified rather than the deacon."[8]

Jesus told this parable: "Two men went into church to pray, one a pastor and the other a convicted murderer. The pastor, standing by himself, was praying, 'God, I thank you that I am not like other people: thieves, cheaters, or even like this murderer. I fast

8. Ridenhour, "Literature."

twice a week and give a tenth of all my income to the church.' But the murderer, standing far off, would not even look up to heaven, but was beating his chest and saying, 'God, be merciful to me, a sinner!' I tell you, this man went down to his home justified rather than the other; for all who praise themselves will be humbled, but all who humble themselves will be praised."

Pounds

(Luke 19:11–27)

"As the people in Jericho were listening to the story about Zacchaeus, Jesus went on to tell a parable, because he was near Jerusalem, and because they supposed that the kingdom of God was to appear immediately. So, he said, 'A state governor went to Washington, DC, to get dictatorial power for himself and then return. He summoned ten of his advisory council members, and gave them one thousand dollars each, and said to them, "Do business with these until I come back." But the citizens of his state hated him and sent a delegation after him, saying, "We do not want this man to have dictatorial power over us." When he returned, having received federal dictatorial power, he ordered the advisory council members, to whom he had given the money, to be summoned so that he might find out what they had gained by trading. The first came forward and said, "Sir, your thousand dollars has made ten thousand more." He said to him, "Well done! Because you have been trustworthy in a small thing, take charge of the taxes of ten cities." Then the second came, saying, 'Sir, your thousand dollars has made five thousand more." He said to him, "And you, take charge of the taxes of five cities." Then the other came, saying, "Sir, here is your thousand dollars. I wrapped it in a piece of cloth and hid it under my bed, for I was afraid of you, because you are a harsh man; you take what you did not deposit, and levy unjust taxes on the people" He said to him, "I will judge you by your own words, you wicked councilman! You knew, did you, that I was a harsh man, taking what I did not deposit and levying unjust taxes on the people? Why then did you not put my money into a bank? Then when I returned, I could have collected it with interest." He said to the bystanders, "Take the thousand dollars from him and give it to the one who has ten thousand dollars." (And they said to him, "Sir, he has ten thousand dollars!") "I tell you, to all those who have more will be given; but from those who have nothing, even what they have will be taken away. But as for these enemies of mine who did not want me be the dictator over them—arrest them, bring them here, and shoot them in my presence."'"

"As the people in Jericho were listening to the story about Zacchaeus, Jesus went on to tell a parable, because he was near Jerusalem, and because they supposed that the kingdom of God was to appear immediately. So, he said, 'A business owner went to another country to acquire another company for himself and then return. He summoned ten of his closest employees, gave them one thousand dollars each, and told them to invest the money until he came back. But his other employees hated him and pressed charges against the owner, saying, "We do not want this man to own the company any longer." When he returned, having acquired another company, he ordered the employees to whom he had given money to come to a meeting so that he might find out what they had gained by trading. The first came forward and said, "Boss! Your money has made another thousand dollars." He said to him, "Well done, faithful employee! Because you have been trustworthy with such a small task, take charge of 50 percent of my new company." Then the second came, saying, "Boss! Your money has made five hundred dollars." He said to him, "And you, manage 25 percent of my new company." Then the other came, saying, "Boss! Here is your money. I buried it in a mason jar, for I was afraid of you, because you are a harsh man; you take what you did not deposit, and reap what you did not sow." He said to him, "I will judge you by your own words, you unreliable employee! You knew, did you, that I was a harsh man, taking what I did not deposit and reaping what I did not sow? Why then did you not put my money into the bank? Then when I returned, I could have collected it with interest." He said to the bystanders, "Take the money and give it to the one who has two thousand dollars." (And they said to him, "Boss, he already has two thousand dollars.") "I tell you, to all those who have, more will be given; but from those who have nothing, even what they have will be taken away. But as for these enemies of mine who did not want me to own this company, fire them immediately and throw them out into the streets.""

Vineyard

(Luke 20:9–16)

Jesus began to tell the people this parable: "A man bought a house, and rented it to tenants, and went to England for a long time. When the first month's rent was due, he sent his rental manager to the tenants in order to collect the rent money that was due; but the tenants beat him and sent him away empty-handed. Next he sent the assistant manager; that one also they beat and insulted and sent away empty-handed. And he sent still a friend; this one also they wounded and threw out of the rental house. Then the owner of the rental house said, 'What shall I do? I will send my beloved son; perhaps they will respect him.' But when the tenants saw him, they discussed it among themselves and said, 'This is the heir to the estate; let us kill him so that the rental house may be ours.' So they threw him out of the rental house and shot him in the back yard. What then will the owner of the rental houses do to them? He will come and have those tenants arrested and removed from his property and give the house to others.' When they heard this, they said, 'Heaven forbid!'"

Jesus began to tell the people this parable: "A man built a condominium, and rented the suites to tenants, and went to Europe for a long time. When the first year's rent was due, he sent his manager to the tenants in order to collect the rent money that was due; but the tenants beat him and sent him away empty-handed. Next he sent the assistant manager; that one also they beat and insulted and sent away empty-handed. And he sent still a friend; this one also they wounded and threw out of the condo. Then the owner of the condo said, 'What shall I do? I will send my beloved son; perhaps they will respect him.' But when the tenants saw him, they discussed it among themselves and said, 'This is the heir to the condo; let us kill him so that the condominium may be ours.' So, they threw him out of the condo and shot him in the maintenance shed. What then will the owner of the rental houses do to them? He will come and have those tenants arrested and removed from his property and give the suites in the condo to others.' When they heard this, they said, 'Heaven forbid!'"

Jesus began to tell the people this parable: "A woman bought an empty lot in a neighborhood and turned it into a community garden; she rented it to tenants, and went to Europe for a long time. When the season came, she sent her manager to the tenants in order to collect her share of the produce of the garden; but the tenants handled her roughly and sent her away empty-handed. Next she sent the assistant manager; that one also they insulted and sent away empty-handed. And she sent still a friend; this one also they wounded and threw out of the garden. Then the owner of the garden said, 'What shall I do? I will send my beloved son; perhaps they will respect him.' But when the tenants saw him, they discussed it among themselves and said, 'This is the heir to the garden lot; let us kill him so that the garden may be ours.' So they threw him out of the garden and shot him in the alley. What then will the owner of the garden do to them? She will come and have those tenants arrested and removed from her property and give the garden to others.' When they heard this, they said, 'Heaven forbid!'"

Fig Tree Revisited

(Luke 21:29–30)

Jesus told a parable: "Look at the oak tree and all the trees; as soon as they sprout leaves, you can see for yourselves and know that summer is already near."

Jesus told a parable: "Look at the apple tree and all the trees; as soon as they blossom, you can see for yourselves and know that spring is already near."

Jesus told a parable: "Look at the maple tree and all the trees; as soon as they sprout leaves, you can see for yourselves and know that summer is already near."

Jesus told a parable: "Look at the maple tree and all the trees; as soon as their leaves become red, yellow, and orange, you can see for yourselves and know that winter is already near."

Jesus told a parable: "Look at the lilies and other perennial flowers planted in the garden; as soon as their bulbs bloom, you can see for yourselves and know that spring is already near."

Jesus told a parable: "Look at the way a person treats servers in a restaurant; when the evening is over, you can see for yourself if the person is kind-hearted or not."

Jesus told a parable: "Look at the moss that forms on a pond; as soon as it grows thick, you can see for yourselves and know that summer is near."

4

Other Parables

Tree King

(Judg 9:8–15)

THE TREES ONCE WENT out to appoint a president for themselves. So they said to the almond tree, "Serve as our president." The almond tree answered them, "Shall I stop producing my rich milk by which lactose-intolerant humans are honored, to go serve as president of the trees?" Then the trees said to apple tree, "You come and serve as our president." But the apple tree answered them, "Shall I stop producing my sweetness and my delicious honey crisp fruit, and go to serve as president of the trees?" Then the trees said to the grape vine, "You come and serve as our president." But the grape vine said to them, "Shall I stop producing my wine that cheers people and becomes the blood of Christ, and go to serve as president of the trees?" So, all the trees said to the thorny honeylocust, "You come and serve as our president." And the thorny honeylocust said to the trees, "If in good faith you are appointing me your president, then come and take refuge in my shade; but if not, let fire come out of the thorny honeylocust and start a forest fire."

The berry bushes once went out to appoint a president for themselves. So they said to the blue berry bush, "Serve as our president." The blue berry bush answered them, "Shall I stop producing my low-calorie, antioxidant, rich purple fruit which humans eat for health, to go serve as president of the bushes?" Then the bushes said to the raspberry bush, "You come and reign over us." But the raspberry bush answered them, "Shall I stop producing my low-calorie, sweet, highly-nutritious, and antioxidant red fruit, and go to serve as president of the bushes?" Then the bushes said to the cranberry bush, "You come and serve as our president." But the cranberry bush said to them, "Shall I stop producing my juice, sauce, jam, and Craisins that cheer people on Thanksgiving and Christmas, and go to serve as president of the bushes?" So, all the bushes said to the holly bush, "You come and serve as our president." And the holly bush said to the bushes, "If in good faith you are appointing me president, then come and take refuge in my shade; but if not, let poison come out of the holly and cause vomiting, diarrhea, and dehydration—like a bush fire."

Ewe Lamb

(2 Sam 12:1–4)

Nathan said: "There were two men in a certain city, the one rich and the other poor. The rich man raised and sold pot-bellied pigs; but the poor man had nothing but one pot-bellied piglet, which he had bought. He brought it up, and it grew up with him and with his children; it used to eat his leftovers, and drink from his bowl, and lie on his lap, and it was like a daughter to him. Now there came an out-of-town friend of the rich man, and he was loath to take one of his own pot-bellied pigs to prepare for the visitor who had come to see him, but he took the poor man's pig, slaughtered it, and prepared it for the guest who came to see him."

Nathan said: "There were two men in a certain city, the one rich and the other poor. The rich man raised thousands of chickens and sold their eggs; but the poor man had nothing but one baby chick, which he had bought. He brought it up, and it grew up with him and with his children; it used to peck at his leftovers, and drink from his bowl, and sit on his lap, and it was like a daughter to him. Now there came an out-of-town friend of the rich man, and he was loath to take one of his own chickens to prepare for the visitor who had come to see him, but he took the poor man's hen, slaughtered it, and prepared it for the guest who came to see him."

Flame, Smoke, Water

(2 Esd 4:47–50)

Uriel said to Ezra: "Stand at my right side, and I will show you the interpretation of a parable." So I stood and looked and lo, a raging forest fire passed by before me, and when the flames had gone by, I looked, and lo, the smoke remained. And after this a tornado (hurricane, water spout) passed before me and poured down a heavy and violent rain, and when the violent rainstorm had passed, drops still remained in the clouds." Uriel said, "Consider it for yourself; for just as the rain is more than the drops, and the fire is greater than the smoke, so the quantity that passed was far greater; but drops and smoke remained."

Uriel said to Ezra: "Stand at my right side, and I will show you the interpretation of a parable." So I stood and looked and lo, a bright beam of sunshine passed by before me, and when the beam had been blocked by clouds, I looked, and lo, the light remained. And after this a fog passed before me and removed all visibility, and when the fog had begun to burn off, shafts of light still remained in the fog." Uriel said, "Consider it for yourself; for just as the sun is more than a beam, and the light is greater than the fog, so the quantity that passed was far greater; but sunshine and light remained."

Uriel said to Ezra: "Stand at my right side, and I will show you the interpretation of a parable." So I stood and looked and lo, a blizzard passed by before me, and when the snowstorm had gone by, I looked, and lo, the snowflakes remained. And after this sleet passed before me and dropped down heavy ice pellets, and when the sleet had passed, rain continued to fall on the earth." Uriel said, "Consider it for yourself; for just as the snow is more than the snowflakes, and the sleet is greater than the rain, so the quantity that passed was far greater; but snowflakes and rain remained."

Clay and Gold

(2 Esdras 8:2)

". . . I will tell you a parable, Ezra. Just as, when you ask the earth, it will tell you that it provides a large amount of clay from which pottery, porcelain, bone china, stoneware, and terra cotta are made, but only a little dust from which gold, platinum, palladium, silver, rhodium, ruthenium, and iridium come, so is the course of the present world.

First Tent

(Heb 9:9)

The Christian church building is a parable of the present time, during which contributions cannot change the conscience of the worshippers.

The Jewish synagogue is a parable of the present time, during which prayers cannot change the conscience of the worshippers.

The Moslem mosque is a parable of the present time, during which prostrations cannot change the conscience of the worshippers.

The Buddhist temple is a parable of the present time, during which chants cannot change the conscience of the adherents.

The Hindu shrine is a parable of the present time, during which offerings placed before a sacred statue of a god or goddess cannot change the conscience of the worshippers.

The Taoist temple is a parable of the present time, during which incense cannot change the conscience of the adherents.

5

Current Parables

One Sentence Parables (Aphorisms)

The kingdom of God is like a man who asked his wife, "In what language is Swan Lake danced?"

The kingdom of heaven is like a child who asked, "What language does the wind speak?"

The kingdom of heaven is like a child who asked, "What language does God speak?"

The kingdom of God is like a musician who asked, "Does the wind notate its music using Gregorian Chant or standard forms of musical notation?"

The empire of God is like a man who learned to dance while standing still!

The kingdom of heaven is like creation still being created.

The kingdom of heaven is like a monk who declared, "Silence is spoken here!"

The reign of God is like a sixth-grader who asked his teacher, "Can a politician change his or her party?"

The reign of God is like a sixth-grader who asked her teacher, "Can a drug lord imprison himself for selling cocaine?"

The kingdom of heaven is like a fifth-grader who asked the security guard, "Can a serial killer turn himself in to the police?"

The reign of God is like a recruit who asked a police offer, "Can a rapist convict himself?"

Those who experience the reign of God know that we change in order to stay the same.

Those who experience the reign of God know that if we ever agreed with two political candidates, we would all be wrong.

The reign of God is like a mother, who, after making her son stand in a corner, told his father, "Do you know what your son said today? When he grows up, he wants to be president!"

The reign of God is like a little girl, who, while kneeling by her bed, told her mother, "God's pretty good about answering my knee-mail!"

The kingdom of God is like a .01 certificate of deposit at three-percent interest.

The reign of God is like a virus; you have to catch it, it is contagious, and it makes you sick.

Knowledge of the kingdom of heaven is contagious; it infects truth.

The kingdom of heaven is like a rancid bag of garbage, which a sanitation worker threw into the garbage truck, and it made the whole vehicle stink!

The kingdom of heaven is like drugs which a pill-pusher gave to three million children until all of them were hooked!

The kingdom of heaven is like money which a rich man took and laundered through three banks until they were all bankrupt.

The kingdom of God is like a sign posted on a tree behind barbed wire: "Please trespass here!"

The kingdom of heaven is like a sign posted on a tree behind a fence: Trespassing permitted here!"

The empire of God is like a sign posted on a tree behind a fence: "Trespassing required!"

The kingdom of God is like a child, who took his parents to court and divorced them.

The kingdom of God is like writing a finite history of infinitude!

The kingdom of heaven is like a thief, who whispered to a judge that he told lies for Jesus.

The reign of God is like anyone who doesn't want to go (die) except in very good used condition.

The kingdom of God is like a tow truck hooked up to a Volkswagen Beetle, which pulled it to the gas station.

The kingdom of heaven is like a sign on a home: "Please rob this house."

The reign of God is like a sign along a highway: "Please litter this area!"

The empire of God is like a sign along a highway: "Rewards given for littering here!"

The kingdom of God is like a woman, who said to her husband, "I like to commute," and he replied, "You work at home!"

The kingdom of heaven is built to last forever, but not ever to be visited.

You've got a great future behind you in the reign of God.

The kingdom of heaven is like a Hindu woman who went to a temple not to see God, but to let God gaze upon her!

Story Parables (Narratives)

The kingdom of God is like one chicken in a coop who said to another one: "They hired a fox to guard us! Personally, I think they're carrying this equal-opportunity employment stuff a bit too far!"

The reign of God is like a misplaced bag of contagious bacteria from a laboratory. It was taken out with the regular garbage and hauled to the city landfill where it burst open and was spread throughout the dump site.

The kingdom of God is like a refrigerator full of donated pints of blood into which an HIV+ (AIDS) man took his Red-Cross-rejected donation and poured his tainted blood on all until it streaked over all the pints of blood with red.

The empire of God is like a sign in a neighborhood: "Children Not at Play, No Fun Zone." One observer stated, "That is how to tell you're in a politically correct neighborhood."

The reign of God is like a soldier who asked his commanding officer, "Does it help to resolve the confrontation between the US and ISIS if we strike back at evil violence with good violence?"

The kingdom of God is like eleven people hanging on a rope under a helicopter; ten of them were men and one of them was a woman. The rope was not strong enough to carry them all, so they decided that one had to leave; otherwise, all were going to fall. The woman gave a very touching speech, saying that she would voluntarily let go of the rope because she was used to giving up everything for her husband and kids. As soon as she finished her little speech, all the men started clapping their hands.

The reign of God is like St. Paul's concept of God. Did it come from the Hebrew Bible (Old Testament) or from Paul's understanding of how God seems to have changed while remaining the same?

Current Parables

The kingdom of God is like the famous artist Georgia O'Keeffe, who said: "I have been absolutely terrified every moment of my life, and I've never let it keep me from doing a single thing I wanted to do."[1]

The kingdom of heaven is like a certain citizen who was arrested by a baron and shut up in a dungeon by a ferocious-looking jailer, who carried a great key. The door of his cell closed with a bang. He lay in the dark dungeon for thirty years. Each day the big door would be opened with a great creaking; water and bread would be brought in and the door closed with a bang again. After thirty years, the prisoner decided that he wanted to die, but he did not want to commit suicide. So, the next day when the jailer came, he decided to attack him, and the jailer would kill him. In preparation he decided he should examine the door, so he turned the handle, and to his amazement the door opened. He found that there was no lock. He groped along the corridor and felt his way upstairs. At the top of the stairs two soldiers were chatting, and they made no attempt to stop him. He crossed the great yard. There was an armed guard on the drawbridge, but he paid no attention to him, and he walked out a free man. He went home unmolested; he realized that he had been a captive, not of stone and iron, but of false belief. He had only thought he was locked in.[2]

The reign of God is like a bishop, who warned the members of his flock about a certain performer, who represented a threat to the morality of the people. He preached against the performer, took out ads against the performer in the local newspaper, posted tweets condemning the performer's values, and repeatedly warned adults of the danger of attending the performer's shows. Despite all his work, the performer's shows were well attended. After leaving town, the performer's manager wrote to the bishop to thank him and enclosed a check for three thousand dollars. He wrote that he was grateful for all the free advertising the bishop provided.[3]

1. Adapted from Helwig, "Materialize Your Visions," 50.
2. Adapted from Fox, *Around the Year*, 210.
3. Adapted from Whitfield, *Crisis of Bad Preaching*, 42.

The kingdom of God is like a lifesaving station on a dangerous seacoast with frequent shipwrecks. The building was originally just a hut, and there was only one boat, but the completely devoted members kept a constant watch over the sea and went out day and night tirelessly searching for the lost. Many were saved by this station, so it became famous. Some of those saved and others in the surrounding areas then gave their time and money to support its work. New boats were bought and crews were trained. The little lifesaving station grew. Time passed. Some members of the lifesaving station became unhappy that the building was so crude and poorly equipped. They felt that a more comfortable place should be provided as the first refuge of those saved from the sea. So they replaced the cots with beds, put in better furniture, and enlarged the building. Soon the lifesaving station became a popular gathering place for its proud members; they redecorated it beautifully and used it as a kind of club. Fewer members were now interested in going to sea on lifesaving missions, so they hired lifeboat crews to do this work. The lifesaving motif still prevailed in the club decorations, however, and there was a liturgical lifeboat in the room where club initiations were held. About this time, a large ship was wrecked off the coast and the hired crews brought in boatloads of cold, wet, half-drowned people. They were dirty, wounded, sick, and some had differently colored skin. The beautiful new club was left untidy and muddy. So the property committee immediately had a shower house built outside the club where shipwreck victims could clean up before coming inside. At the next meeting there was a split in the club membership. Some leaders wanted to stop the club's lifesaving activities, seeing them as an unpleasant hindrance to the normal social life of the club. Some of the members insisted that lifesaving was their primary purpose. But they were voted down and told that if they wanted to save the various people shipwrecked on those waters, they could start their own lifesaving station down the coast. They did. But as the years went by the new station experienced the same changes that had occurred in the old. It evolved into a club, and yet another lifesaving station was founded. History continued to repeat itself, and if you visit that seacoast today, you find a number of exclusive clubs along that shore. Shipwrecks are still frequent in those waters, but most of the people drown.[4]

"In 1996, in northern Uganda, the government placed 1.5 million residents in 'protective villages' that were really containment camps. Many Ugandans still live there in small huts about eight to ten feet apart with eight water holes per thirty thousand people. A painful part of their twelve-year civil war has been the massive abduction of children, turning little boys into young soldiers, in some cases sent to kill their own parents, and turning little girls into sex slaves. . . . Now that there's a truce in Uganda, many young girls are returning with small children born during their ten years of abduction. A refugee resettlement employee asked the elders, 'What will happen to the young girls coming home?' One elder quickly said that if a girl had run off and returned pregnant, she would be cast out of the village. This was their tribal law. But the question was put by one Ugandan elder wizened by his captivity: 'And what will we do when ten thousand of our children, abducted and abused, return with a generation of our grandchildren fathered by our enemies?' One of the elders stared off, another cried. And in the incubation of that painful silence, a new form of thinking arose that would bring the children home."[5]

4. Adapted from Jezreel, "A Parable for Parishes," 26.
5. Adapted from Nepo, "Our Walk," 97–98.

Bibliography

The Access Bible: New Revised Standard Version. New York: Oxford University Press, 1999.

Auer, Jim. "The Darnel and the Tares." *Liguorian* (March 1997) 38–43.

Ben-Shahar, Tal. "Five Questions with Tal Ben-Shahar." *Spirituality & Health* 21:6 (2018) 104.

The Contemporary English Version. Nashville: Nelson, 1995.

Dryer, Elizabeth A. "God only Knows." *U.S. Catholic* 63:9 (1998) 41–42.

Encarta: World English Dictionary. New York: St. Martin, 1999.

"Etcetera: Parable Update." *Salt of the Earth* (May/June 1997) 34.

Fox, Emmet. *Around the Year with Emmet Fox*. New York: HarperCollins, 1992.

Galson, David. "Dispatches." *The Fourth R* 32:1 (2019) 29.

Griffin, Douglas L. "Reading the Bible as Theological Fiction." *The Fourth R* 33:1 (2020) 5–8, 20.

Hall, Kenley D. "Jesus: God's Story and Storyteller." *Ministry: International Journal for Pastors* 91:11 (2019) 10–13.

Helwig, Terry. "Materialize Your Visions." *Spirituality & Health* 7:4 (2004) 48–51.

Jezreel, Jack. "A Parable for Parishes." *U.S. Catholic* 84:9 (2019) 25–27.

McGinnis, Kimberly. "Literature and World of the New Testament" taught by Mark G. Boyer. Springfield, MO: Southwest Missouri State University, Fall Semester 1991.

Miller, Robert J. "Inside(r)s and Outside(r)s." *The Fourth R* 33:1 (2020) 9–12, 24.

Nepo, Mark. "Our Walk in the World." *Spirituality & Health* 21:6 (2018) 97–98.

The New Testament: St. Paul Catholic Edition. New York: Society of St. Paul, 2000.

O'Loughlin, Thomas. *Eating Together, Becoming One*. Collegeville, MN: Liturgical, 2019.

Rayas, Fernando. "Discipleship Demands that We Cross All Kinds of Borders." *U.S. Catholic* 83:12 (2018) 35–37.

Ridenhour. Shane. "Literature and World of the New Testament" taught by Mark G. Boyer. Springfield, MO: Southwest Missouri State University, Fall Semester 1991.

Bibliography

Rohr, Richard. "Loving the Presence in the Present." Center for Action and Contemplation. October 29, 2018. https://cac.org/loving-the-presence-in-the-present-2018-10-29/.

———. "Many Ways of Knowing." Center for Action and Contemplation. January 8, 2019. https://cac.org/many-ways-of-knowing-2019–11-08/.

Scott, Bernard Brandon. "Living in a Re-Imagined World." *The Fourth R* 14:5 (2001) 15–19.

Toth, Vanessa. "Literature and World of the New Testament" taught by Mark G. Boyer. Springfield, MO: Southwest Missouri State University, Fall Semester 1991.

Whitfield, Joshua J. *The Crisis of Bad Preaching.* Notre Dame, IN: Ave Maria, 2019.

Windley-Daust, Susan. "A Literature of Encounter? Reading the Theology of the Body Audiences as Parable and Poem." *Listening: Journal of Communication Ethics, Religion, and Culture* 53:1 (2018) 6–17.

Recent Books
Published by Wipf & Stock

By Mark G. Boyer and Corbin S. Cole

Love Addict

By Mark G. Boyer

Nature Spirituality: Praying with Wind, Water, Earth, Fire

A Spirituality of Ageing

Weekday Saints: Reflections on Their Scriptures

Human Wholeness: A Spirituality of Relationship

A Simple Systematic Mariology

Praying Your Way through Luke's Gospel and the Acts of the Apostles

An Abecedarian of Animal Spirit Guides: Spiritual Growth through Reflections on Creatures

Overcome with Paschal Joy: Chanting through Lent and Easter— Daily Reflections with Familiar Hymns

Taking Leave of Your Home: Moving in the Peace of Christ

An Abecedarian of Sacred Trees: Spiritual Growth through Reflections on Woody Plants

Recent Books Published by Wipf & Stock

Divine Presence: Elements of Biblical Theophanies

Fruit of the Vine: A Biblical Spirituality of Wine

Names for Jesus: Reflections for Advent and Christmas

Talk to God and Listen to the Casual Reply: Experiencing the Spirituality of John Denver

Christ Our Passover Has Been Sacrificed: A Guide through Paschal Mystery Spirituality—Mystical Theology in The Roman Missal

Rosary Primer: The Prayers, The Mysteries, and the New Testament

From Contemplation to Action: The Spiritual Process of Divine Discernment Using Elijah and Elisha as Models

All Things Mary: Honoring the Mother of God—An Anthology of Marian Reflections

Shhh! The Sound of Sheer Silence: A Biblical Spirituality that Transforms

What is Born of the Spirit is Spirit: A Biblical Spirituality of Spirit

Very Short Reflections—for Advent and Christmas, Lent and Easter, Ordinary Time, and Saints—through the Liturgical Year

www.ingramcontent.com/pod-product-compliance
Lightning Source LLC
Chambersburg PA
CBHW060311100426
42812CB00003B/745